S0-CGR-891

KETO AFTER 50

KETO FOR SENIORS - 5G NET OF CARBS, 30 MINUTE MEALS | LOSE WEIGHT, RESTORE BONE HEALTH AND FIGHT DISEASE FOREVER

Teresa Baker

Teresa Baker

KETO AFTER 50

INCLUDES RECIPE INDEX, NUTRITIONAL FACTS, AND SCORE POINTS GRADING

✓ **EASE OF COOKING**

✓ **AVAILABILITY OF INGREDIENTS**

✓ **SPEED OF PREPARATION**

✓ **BUDGET FRIENDLY**

✓ **MEAL PREP FRIENDLY**

✓ **GROCERY EFFICIENT**

✓ **ALSO GLUTEN FREE, DIABETIC & PALEO FRIENDLY**

BoldBar Publishing

Copyright ©2019

All rights reserved. Except as permitted under the U.S. Copyright Act of 1976, the scanning, uploading and distribution of this book via the internet or via any other means without the express permission of the author is illegal and punishable by law. Please purchase only authorized electronic and paperback editions, and do not participate in, or encourage electronic piracy of copyrighted material.

Disclaimer

This publication is designed to provide competent and reliable information regarding the subject matter covered. However, it is sold with the understanding that the author is not engaged in rendering professional or nutritional advice. Laws and practices often vary from state to state and country to country and if medical or other expert assistance is required, the services of a professional should be sought. The author specifically disclaims any liability that is incurred from the use or application of the contents of this book.

Teresa Baker

You May Also Like ...

Book Cover	Book Title	Purchase Link
	Keto Desserts Cookbook 2019 *Easy, Quick and Tasty High-Fat Low-Carb Ketogenic Treats to Try from No-bake Energy Bomblets to Sugar-Free Creamsicle Melts and beyond*	**Buy on Amazon**
	Keto Diet for Beginners 2020 *The Definitive Ketogenic Diet Guide to Kick-start High Level Fat burning, Weight Loss & Healthy Lifestyle in 2020 and Beyond.*	**Buy on Amazon**
	Keto Breakfast Cookbook *Simple No-Mess, No-Fuss Ketogenic Meals to Prepare, Boost Morning Metabolism and Ramp Up Your Energy!*	**Buy on Amazon**
	Keto Lunch Cookbook *Easy Ketogenic Recipes for Work and School; Low Carb Meals to Prep, Grab and Go	With Q&A, Tips, and More..*	**Buy on Amazon**

Note that the Kindle Editions of these books will be made available to you for **FREE** when you get the paperback editions from the Amazon USA store

CONTENTS

WHAT IS THIS BOOK ALL ABOUT?

This book contains proven steps and strategies, on how to start preparing healthy Keto meals if you're over the age of 50 and want to lose weight, reverse disease and live healthy. This book offers unique Keto recipes that are completely sugar-free, gluten-free and healthy. In this book, you will find several tips, tricks and strategies on how to get started and stay keto-adapted.

This Book comes structured in two Parts: Part 1 explains the basics of the Keto diet, why you should get started on Keto after 50, how to meal prep recipes and tips for success on Keto after age 50. Part 2 features loads of keto recipes that you can tweak in many ways for a variety of flavors. Each recipe has a nutrient content guide per serving. Finally, it also contains a quick guide measurement conversion table that can come in handy when preparing your recipes. Prepare and enjoy these recipes while spending quality and enjoyable time with your family and friends. Teresa's tips also make it easy for anyone to get started and will guide you in ways to quickly achieve success on the Keto diet.

Without further ado, let's get started!

Specifically, in this cutting edge book, you'll learn:

- Supposedly regular Keto-friendly foods you should be avoiding if you're over 50
- How to deal with the Keto flu and engage your body to heal and recover faster and better
- How to limit carb cravings, emotional eating, binges and occasional cheating
- 2important secrets why restricting calorie is a must for you at age 50+
- How Aging Affects Your Health and what it means for You on Keto
- How Keto Can Help you with weight loss, improved brain and memory function After 50
- How to heal your body completely with special tips never taught anywhere

Also in this guide, you'll discover:

- ✓ A Custom-fit way to try Keto in a specific way with added bonus
- ✓ List of foods you should never eat, even if they are the holy grail of regular Keto diets
- ✓ 10 Best Supplements you should be taking if you're on Keto and over 50
- ✓ 6 Supplements you should never take
- ✓ 10 Best health-supporting and disease-fighting foods you should be eating everyday on Keto
- ✓ 10 foods you should never miss out on, even if you have no time to cook
- ✓ Best Ways to stay on track the Keto diet, track ketosis and track Calories
- ✓ Top Proven ways to reap all the benefits of Keto after age 50

Even if you suffer from high blood sugar levels, food addictions, binge or emotional eating, you can begin to see great results from a tailored Keto that caters specifically to your needs

You will also discover Keto recipes that are:

- Quick, Easy and Simple to Prepare

- Under 30 minute meals
- 5g net of carbs
- Simple, precise, and defined preparation instructions
- Budget-friendly and very affordable
- Highly delicious and sugar-free wide range of recipes
- Gluten-Free, Diabetic and Paleo friendly
- Easily available ingredients

Teresa Baker

INTRODUCTION

As the world gets more polluted and obesity-related disorders get to epidemic proportions, people are becoming more health-conscious. We now know that stress, unhealthy eating habits, and sedentary lifestyle all contribute to obesity and we are constantly searching for new ways to maintain a healthy weight.

Keto diet first appeared in the 1920s as a treatment for reducing epileptic seizures in children. However, it also turned out to successfully starve cancer cells and help with cellular healing. Besides, recent studies suggest that the Ketogenic diet has a range of neurological benefits that could help patients with autism, Parkinson's, Alzheimer's, etc. However, it was only in 2012 that the Keto diet took the world by storm when it became apparent that following this diet was the quickest way to lose weight. Although the Keto lifestyle has gained popularity all over the world, many controversies still surround the diet. What's so special about it? Is it safe after 50? In what way would it be beneficial?

Modern eating habits are the main reason we are so unhealthy - we eat much more than we need, we eat all the time, and we eat unhealthy foods. On top of that, our sedentary lifestyles make it impossible to use all the calories we ingest through food and the body turns them into fat. As a result, a huge proportion of the population, especially in the most developed countries, is overweight or obese.

There are many reasons unhealthy eating habits have become a global trend:

➤ Thanks to modern agriculture practices, food is plentiful and cheap.

➤ Agriculture is a million-dollar business and aggressive marketing campaigns encourage people to eat a lot, eat all the time, and eat processed foods.

➤ Processed foods are very unhealthy but unfortunately, they are usually very tasty, because they are full of salt, sugar, and flavor additives

With this in mind, it's not surprising that the diet industry has become a booming business. We all want to look better, live longer, and be healthier and almost the first thing you think of when you look at your body in a swimsuit is that you should start dieting.

There are many different kinds of diets and just as many reasons people diet, e.g. to lose weight, to prevent disease, to lower blood pressure, etc. However, not all diets are made equal. Some are expensive, complicated, or for one reason or another, difficult to stick to for a long time.

Although the Keto diet was first used in 1920 as an alternative treatment for children's epileptic seizures, it soon turned out it was an excellent diet for weight loss. And although most people start losing weight almost immediately, not everyone finds this diet easy.

CHAPTER 1

BACKGROUND

After all said and done about the Ketogenic diet, have you ever wondered if the diet has benefits for older adults? If yes, in what way? Well, yes, the Ketogenic diet has great benefits for people over the age of 50. Since the science behind the diet emphasizes calorie restriction, it is no surprise that Keto has immense benefits for aging given that calorie and carb restriction increases longevity and slows down the process of aging.

Since research has shown that the Keto diet can improve cognitive decline, limit risk for type 2 diabetes and similar health conditions, it becomes important that you approach Keto bearing these in mind. The majority of your carbs should be replaced by fats and these fats should be about 70 to 80% of your total calorie intake. Limit Carbs to not more than 5% while proteins should be about 10 to 20%. Your body will go into Ketosis because you are forcing your body to utilize fats for energy production rather than glucose which is mainly sourced from carbs. Your body utilizes Ketones as an alternate fuel source when in Ketosis. Ketones are molecules produced from fats in the liver when there is a limit in glucose (as a result of limited carbs, since glucose is derived from carbs)

Most people avoid fat due to its high calorie content, but never believe the lie – yes, we've been lied to all along for a long time. New evidence has proven that Keto diet type rather than low-fat diets are effective for promoting weight loss. Also, Keto diets increase satiety and reduce hunger pangs which are important when you intend to lose weight.

It is not a hard thing to switch to a Keto diet after age 50. Of course, they may be challenges, especially with the transition – such as Keto flu, but once you understand your body, know its needs and know what to do, it become quite easier.

For starters, the simple formula is to increase the protein and fat content in your meals and snacks while reducing the carbs, but it is not all black and white. Keto after 50 must be made custom-fit, with specific adjustments according to age, body weight and activity levels. It also helps to adjust as your body responds to it. While you must restrict your carb intake to reach and remain in Ketosis, you must be particularly mindful of the kind of carbs.

Different people achieve Ketosis with varying amounts of carb intake. Generally, it is easy to reach and stay in Ketosis when you decrease your carb intake to 10%. That being said, your best approach to losing weight on a Keto diet after 50, is to stick with Keto-friendly foods and avoid carb-rich foods.

The Ketogenic diet is similar to the Atkins and the Low-Carb diets – on the bases that they are all very low-carb and high-fat diets. In each diet, you have to consume more fats than carbohydrates. Your body goes into a metabolic state (known as Ketosis) because the carb content in your diet is drastically reduced. During Ketosis, your body efficiently turns *fat into Ketones* in the liver, acting as a source of energy, especially to your brain.

Besides increasing the Ketones levels in your body, one other benefit of the Ketogenic diet is the massive reduction in blood sugar levels in your body.

Ever wonder...

- Why the Keto diet is effective for overall health improvement including weight loss?

- How exactly the Keto diet works to help the body burn fat rather than carbohydrates for fuel?

If yes, then, here is your answer.

When you eat a meal containing lots of carbs, your body must convert the carbs to glucose. Your body's main source of energy when you consume a carb-rich meal is glucose. Then, insulin must move the glucose to your bloodstream. In contrast, a Keto diet contains low amounts of carbs. Thus, your body needs another source of fuel. This new source of fuel is fats. Since carbs are literally low or absent, the liver converts fatty acids contained in fats to Ketone bodies (also called Ketones). This is a basic summary of the Ketosis process.

When fatty acids are broken down, three Ketone bodies are produced in the following order:

- Acetoacetate ⟶ Beta-HydroxyButyric Acid (BHB) ⟶ Acetone

The macros for the best and standard Keto diets should be 70% fats, 20% protein, and 10% carbs.

When you're on a Keto diet, you really do not need to watch your protein intake. Gluconeogenesis, a metabolic process in your body is responsible for generating glucose from other non-carb sources such as protein, glycerol, and lactate.

With gluconeogenesis, your body can;

- Fuel some tissues that do not directly use Ketones. These tissues include testicles, red blood cells, and certain parts of the brain.

- maintain the right levels of blood glucose

- generate glycogen

As a result, it is impossible for Ketosis to occur without gluconeogenesis (GNG). Although, they are an awesome source of energy, Ketones can only fuel some of the body tissues while GNG fuels the rest of them. You can't possibly get kicked out of Ketosis despite an increase in your GNG rate when you consume more protein macros than the allowable Keto macros because GNG is a highly stable and regulatory mechanism. So, with that in mind, the benefits of a Keto diet are way beyond calorie restriction because on a cellular level:

- Using Ketones improves mitochondrial function and production

- Your body generates *less reactive* oxygen species when you burn Ketones for fuel

- Carbohydrate limitation activates anti-inflammatory and autophagy processes.

Adapting to Keto

The first time you try running your body on Ketones, you will likely experience some side effects, commonly called the "Keto flu". But over time, your body will become adapted and will prefer fat for energy. So, it is important to give your body some time to adjust and become adapted before coming to conclusions.

One of the ways to do this is by regular checking of your Ketone levels. By checking your Ketone levels frequently, you can ensure your Ketogenic diet is effective, maintain the state of Ketosis, and compare progress with the diet.

Getting into Ketosis

The absolute best way to know that you've entered (and still) in Ketosis is to test your Ketone levels. When your body enters Ketosis and burns fat for fuel, it will create Ketones which goes into your breath, blood and urine. You can check your Ketone levels by testing your urine, breath and blood levels using any of these methods:

1. **Blood Testing**

Blood testing is the best indicator for monitoring Ketone levels in your body. You can use a blood glucose meter with a blood strip to check. However, if you test constantly, this method can be quite expensive. For optimum results, ensure you consume diets rich in healthy fats, proteins, vitamin, and minerals.

2. **Breath Testing**

By using a breath meter, you can test the acetone levels in your breath. The acetone level is an indication of the Ketone levels in your breath. Unlike urine strips, there are no ongoing costs associated with using a breath meter. You only have to purchase it one time.

Based on experience, this test isn't 100% effective and so, you shouldn't rely on it alone to for Ketone testing.

3. **Urine Testing**

There are urine strips (available at your local drugstore) that show your Ketone levels via color change indication. However, if you've been in Ketosis for some time, urine testing isn't always reliable. By being more efficient with your body's use of Ketones, there can be an indication of lower levels of Ketones. Hydration and electrolyte levels in your body can also influence the reading.

The Ketogenic diet is a low-carb, high-fat diet and moderate-protein diet which revolve around ketones and ketosis. To function well, your body needs energy. Carbs are easiest to burn, so this is what your body will burn first when you deprive it of food. However, when it uses all the carbs, it will start burning fat, and that's when you start losing weight.

To get your body to start burning fat, you first have to get yourself into ketosis. You can reach ketosis by fasting; however, starving yourself is not the easiest way to maintain a healthy weight. You can achieve the same result by following the Keto diet.

When you first go on a low-carb diet, you may struggle for the first few days as your body attempts to get used to the new eating regimen. Don't be alarmed if you experience mild discomfort, such as a headache or fatigue.

The easiest way to reach ketosis and start burning fat is to follow the key principles of the Ketogenic lifestyle.

8 Steps to Reaching Ketosis:

1)   Restrict carbohydrates in your diet

2)   Limit protein intake

3)   Increase fat intake

4)   Drink water

5)   Stop snacking

6)   Try intermittent fasting

7)   Exercise

8)   Take supplements

So, how will you know you're in ketosis?

The easiest way to check if you've reached ketosis is to have your urine or blood checked with urine or blood strips. Alternatively, look for telltale signs and symptoms of ketosis:

6 Signs you're in Ketosis:

1. Dry mouth
2. Bad breath
3. Loss of appetite
4. Increased energy
5. Loss of weight
6. Stronger urine smell

Debunking the Myths: What Keto Really Means for you after 50

With so many different diets all promising miraculous weight loss, it's no wonder many people are skeptical about Keto and believe it's just another fad diet. The main problem is that many of these "healthy" diets come with conflicting information about what's safe to eat and what isn't. Besides, the Keto diet is unusual in that, it is based on the increased fat intake so many myths are circulating around this way of eating.

Debunking the nutrition myths is important because they can sabotage your weight-loss efforts, give you false hope or make you force a certain dietary regimen upon yourself that may cause more harm than good.

5 Most Common Keto Diet Myths:

1. **Keto diet is a long-term solution**

A balanced Keto diet plan will provide all the nutrients your body needs to function well, but even so, this diet is not meant to be followed forever. The main reason you shouldn't stay on this diet for long is that it is low in protein so the longer you stick to it, the greater the chance of muscle loss.

Besides, a prolonged Keto diet may slow your metabolism so after a couple of months on this diet you may find that your body is burning fewer calories than it did when you first started dieting. Therefore, nutritionists recommend that although this diet will help you shed pounds quickly, you should not follow it for more than three months.

2.   You can only have 10 grams of carbs a day

There is a lot of debate about how much carbs one is allowed to take to reach ketosis. There are claims that only 10g a day is all you can take, but researchers say that as long as you take less than 50g of carbs a day, you will continue to lose weight. The trick with sticking to a low carb diet is to know where the "hidden" carbs come from. In other words, there is no point in eliminating bread and pasta from your diet if you drink Coke, Starbucks latte, Red Bull or use sweets, cereals, health bars, salad dressings, sauces, and fruits.

3.   You can eat any type of fat

While on a Keto diet, about 75% of your calories should come from fats, but these have to be healthy fats, e.g. olive oil, coconut oil, butter, nuts and seeds, nut butters, fish, grass-fed meat, eggs, and avocado.

Trans fats to avoid are those that come from foods such as bacon, sausages, ham, French fries, pastry and cakes, deep-fried fast foods, margarine, processed snack foods, etc. When you use only healthy fats, you will not only lose weight more quickly, but lower the risk of cardiovascular disease.

4.   Keto diet is high in protein

To stay in ketosis and avoid ketoacidosis, you must reduce, rather than increase, your protein intake. To know how much protein you should take, you need to know your macros, i.e. the nutritional requirements based on your age, gender, and occupation. However, it is potentially very dangerous depriving yourself of protein because protein is very important for a healthy brain function, body repair, and muscle mass. Understand this - you will do less damage to your Keto diet plan if you take more protein than you should than if you don't take enough. It is carbs that can interfere with your ketosis, not the proteins. So, regardless of how desperate you are to lose weight, make sure you take some protein every day.

5.   Keto diet means no alcohol consumption

Although you can drink alcohol while following the Keto diet, it should be only low carb alcoholic drinks and you should only take them in moderation.

You CAN drink hard liquor (e.g. vodka, rum, gin, brandy, and whiskey), dry wine, and light beer.

You CAN'T drink mixed drinks (e.g. margarita, vermouth, and anything containing sweeteners), sweet wines (e.g. Riesling, Moscato, port, sherry, etc.), liqueurs, ciders, sangrias, as well as all drinks mixed with soda or juice.

CHAPTER 2

KNOW YOUR MACROS

Do You Know Your Macros? What it means for you after 50

The term "macros" is short for macronutrients and it refers to nutrients essential for optimal health. Macros provide energy and stamina and are found in:

- Carbohydrates

There are different opinions on how much carbs you can take and still get your body to burn fat and the recommendations vary from 10 grams to 50 grams per day. The fewer carbs you take, the faster you'll lose weight, but carbs provide energy so you need to make sure you take enough to keep yourself going throughout the day. Limited carb intake is the main reason most people can't stay on Keto for very long.

- Protein

Proteins are building blocks of your body and they are essential for healthy muscles, cell formation, tissue maintenance, and are the main source of physical strength. Although the Keto diet requires that you limit your protein intake, you should never go without protein for you risk losing muscle mass. The best source of protein is meat, fish, eggs, dairy, beans, tofu, etc. On average, one should take about 100 grams of protein per day.

- Fats

Healthy fats are where your calories come from on a Keto diet and these should be taken from olive oil, coconut oil, avocado, heavy cream, nuts and seeds, etc. This is probably the most difficult aspect of the Keto diet for people to understand because until relatively recently, most healthy diets insisted that fats should be avoided.

What we didn't know thirty years ago is that there is a major difference between healthy and unhealthy fats. Essential fats are necessary for proper thyroid and adrenal activity, hormone production, liver function, brain development, breakdown of cholesterol, etc. Besides, some of the healthy fats contain antioxidants which help destroy free radicals.

The number of macros you need for optimal health depends on your age, gender, and occupation. However, although while on the Keto diet you are expected to reduce the amount of both carbs and protein, depriving yourself of these nutrients comes with many negative side-effects, such as loss of muscle mass, slower metabolism, and disrupted sleep.

To work out your personal macros you can use some of the different formulas available. However, generally speaking, if you weigh about 80 kg (176 lbs), are under 30, and lead a sedentary lifestyle, you probably have about 20% body fat. To get rid of it, you should take about 100 grams of protein, 15 to 20 grams of carbs, and 80 grams of fat per day. This comes to about 1200 calories per day which will support your fat loss.

Keto for Women vs Men

We all know that there are considerable physiological differences between men and women. As a result, their nutritional requirements and the ease with which they maintain healthy weight are also very different. This may sound unfair, but there are very real, evolutionary reasons why women don't lose weight as easily as men.

Although the Keto diet may be one of the quickest ways to lose weight, it is not the easiest. Not all women do well on this diet and some may even gain weight. Besides, your genetic make-up may make it easy or difficult to benefit from dieting. This explains why the Keto diet doesn't work for everyone and why, despite all your efforts, you may not be able to shed those pounds.

3 Reasons Why Women Don't Lose Weight As Easily As Men:

Physiological make-up

Evolutionary, women were created to bear children, so they naturally have more body fat and less muscle mass than men. Muscle burns more calories than fat, so, as soon as men start dieting, they start losing weight. Women take longer because they have more fat to get rid of.

Menopause

During menopause, your metabolism slows down and pounds collect especially around your waist. So, regardless of which diet you are on, during menopause, it's much more difficult to maintain a healthy weight.

Menstruation

During the monthly cycle, women tend to have more cravings, weigh more, have digestion problems, and often get headaches or cramps – or both. All this makes Keto dieting difficult.

To cope with the Keto diet during "these" days, you should eat yogurt, refrain from meat as it takes longer to digest, avoid or reduce cheese and peanut butter, and take Omega-3 supplements. And, if you crave sweets you can take dark chocolate (70% minimum) because it has fewer carbs.

Stress hormones levels

Weight gain is all about hormones and metabolism and it seems that the reason that women, especially those over 50, have a hard time dieting is a hormone-related dysfunction. What's at the root of this dysfunction is the disrupted interaction of the hypothalamus, the pituitary gland, and the adrenal glands. The so-called HPA axis is a major neuroendocrine system that, amongst other things, controls reactions to stress. When their response to stress is disrupted, women often try to cope by indulging in comfort eating, which is another reason why weight gain is easy.

As nutrition science develops and grows, we learn that dieting is more complicated than most people realize. We are all different and our metabolic rate often depends more on our body composition and size than on the food we eat. Instead of forcing yourself to eat in a way that doesn't agree with you, look for alternative dietary plans that may be just what your body needs to get into perfect shape.

5 Things to Bear in Mind if Considering Going on a Keto Diet

1.   Understand what the Keto diet is about

Try to learn as much as you can about Keto lifestyle so you know what you're getting into.

2.   Know your nutritional requirements

Your dietary requirements depend on your age, gender, and occupation and although your goal is to lose weight, you still need to make sure you eat a balanced diet. Be particularly careful if the diet you are about to adopt is drastically different from the way you've been eating until now. If you're used to junk food or if you eat lots of carbs, Keto diet may be a real challenge.

3.   Consider your overall health

If you have a chronic medical condition or are on medication, make sure you discuss the Keto diet with your medical practitioner BEFORE you embark on it.

4.   Set goals

A new way of eating is often challenging and there may be days when you wonder if all the trouble is worth it. This is why it may be a good idea to set a goal because even the most challenging task is easier to handle if you know why you are doing it.

5.   Make a diet plan

Depending on what your current eating habits are like, the Keto diet may be so different from the way you're used to eating that you may have to spend some time figuring out what you are allowed to eat on this diet and how to prepare healthy meals. Fortunately, keto meals are usually very easy to prepare, and you can find the recipes in this book easy to get started with, although some the ingredients you'll need for this diet may be different from what you usually stock your fridge with. Therefore, make a weekly meal plan for breakfast, lunch, snacks, and dinner menus.

Although a balanced diet should include all the nutrients your body needs to function well, while dieting, you should also take into account your age and overall health. Your body undergoes considerable changes as it develops and matures, and a healthy diet can make the transitions easier as well as prevent the onset of many disorders which come with old age.

So, is a low-carb, low-protein diet safe if you're over 50? In the *Keto Diet After 50,* you'll find out why post-menopausal nutritional requirements change and how Keto can help you lose weight quickly while staying healthy and fit.

Importance of Calorie Restriction: How it Slows down Aging

Research has proven that indeed restricting calories has a profound effect on the body's aging mechanism. This can be explained in the way that βOHB, the body's main source of energy when you go into fasting or exercise, blocks a group of enzymes responsible for actively promoting oxidative stress.

Oxidative stress is more or less a by-product of the body's use of oxygen to produce energy. It occurs when the body cells burn oxygen to produce fuel for energy. However, as the body does this, it also produces chemically harmful substances - called free radicals. These free radicals are the major culprits in aging and disease causation as they promote cell damage.

Over time, as the cells continue to produce more and freer radicals, they become less effective in clearing them - leading to a vicious cycle of more oxidative stress, cell damage, aging, and disease.

CHAPTER 3

HOW AGING AFFECTS YOUR NUTRITIONAL NEEDS

Although a diet rich in nutrient-dense foods is recommended for everyone regardless of their age, the nutritional requirements of the human body change as they move through different life stages. Most people think that only young people, ie those whose bodies are still developing, need a lot of nutrients. However, nutritional needs increase after menopause. For example, while younger women need only 1000 milligrams of calcium a day, after menopause, they should take 1,200 milligrams daily.

What happens to your body after 50?

After menopause, many women put on weight mainly because their estrogen levels drop and this can lead to oxidative stress, heart disease, and cancer.

Due to hormone-related changes, menopausal women usually lose muscle mass and their bones become thin and brittle which is why their diets should be rich in calcium. Their needs for vitamin D increase as it improves calcium absorption and helps prevent bone fractures, although too much of it is known to cause kidney stones and constipation.

Unfortunately, most women don't get enough nutrients from their diets, mainly because as they age, they tend to eat less. So, if you have a poor appetite, unhealthy eating habits or simply don't have time to plan and prepare healthy meals, you can overcome many of the deficiencies common to menopausal women by taking supplements.

6 Tips on How to Maintain Good Health After 50:

1.   **Make sure you eat a balanced diet**

Your diet should be nutrient-dense, rather than energy-dense, so make sure your meals are based on eggs, lean meats, fish, dairy, nuts & seeds, legumes, fruit and vegetables, and wholegrain products. Fruit and vegetables are rich in antioxidants that can beat cancer.

Between the ages of 50 and 70, you need about 1,200 milligrams of calcium daily and you can get it from sardines, salmon, broccoli, and kale. Oily fish and vitamin D fortified foods help with the absorption of calcium.

2.   Avoid or limit foods high in energy and low in nutrients

These foods are usually what we snack on, eg cakes, biscuits, soft drinks, energy bars, etc.

3.   Improve your bowel health

The easiest way to do this is by taking fiber-rich foods, especially fresh fruit and vegetables.

4.   Improve your bone health

Try to spend at least 30 minutes outside to benefit from the Sun. Walking or weight-training is a great way to exercise because it strengthens the bones and helps you maintain healthy body weight. However, if you hate exercising and have a poor appetite, make sure that what little food you take is nutrient-rich and contains all the micronutrients your body needs.

5.   Manage the menopausal symptoms with your diet, not medication

A diet rich in phytoestrogens is known to reduce many menopausal symptoms, such as hot flushes. Foods that can help you boost phytoestrogens are tofu, soy milk, and flaxseeds.

6.   Manage your blood pressure

Limit the use of salt.

How Aging Affects Your Health

Nutrient deficiencies:

As we age and grow older, our bodies become less effective and efficient in absorbing specific nutrients from food. As a result, we often have higher deficiencies in nutrients such as Calcium, Iron, Vitamin B12, Vitamin D, and Fats.

It is no surprise then that many common symptoms associated with aging are actually symptoms of deficiency of some of these nutrients. For example, a calcium deficiency is common with problems of the bone and heart health. Iron deficiency leads to symptoms of chronic fatigue, brain fog and loss of concentration. Deficiency in Vitamin D and fats can lead to problems with skin, hair, vision, memory, and heart.

Bone health:

Osteoporosis, a condition where the bones become brittle, fragile and less dense is a common problem amongst seniors. This is because as you age, the body becomes less effective in assimilating Calcium. So even if you meet your recommended daily intake of Calcium via dairy intake, your body may not be able to efficiently absorb and utilize it and this becomes a concern for many people over 50.

So, it is important to consider special factors as this as you try Keto especially as regards dairy-rich Keto meals and see the best and most effective approach to success in Keto when you're over 50.

What helps in this scenario, is to look for ways to limit interference with Calcium absorption as against increasing consumption of more milk.

Note: You don't necessarily need to increase dairy intake at this age. Here is why.

Research has shown that countries with the highest prevalence of Osteoporosis also have the highest rates of dairy consumption.

So, it is better to focus on ways to cut off interference with calcium absorption and one of the best ways to do this is to reduce or eliminate toxins from our bodies and diet. It also helps to have a Keto rich meal rich in varied micronutrients.

In this light, a Keto diet that is:

- low in toxins

- rich in micronutrients, not just a specific macronutrient such as calcium

- has the right balance of macros

- has lower amounts of protein and protein-rich foods will definitely be better to focus on.

Insulin resistance:

Many senior citizens in our society are overweight and dealing with insulin-related conditions like diabetes. This is serious, as diabetes can lead to things like vision loss, kidney disease, and more.

The high-quality sources of animal protein on the Ketogenic diet can easily account for excellent sources of these important nutrients.

Importance of Keto for Aging

Keto isn't just a diet, it's a lifestyle. The Ketogenic diet provides great dietary value both for optimum health and weight loss. For every calorie count, the kero diet provides a great amount of nutrition.

This is fundamental because the basic amount of calories needed for daily survival is lower for older adults than it is for other age groups. However, seniors still need the same amount of nutrients as younger people. So, this is where Keto comes into play, as no other diet provides as much nutrient-dense food per calorie as the Keto diet.

If you do not suffer from any profound medical issues, the Keto diet can still be beneficial to you. This is because it can cause:

1. **An improvement in body fat composition**

The Keto diet can be perfect for you either to gain muscle mass or lose fat. With a carbohydrate-restriction diet, you can drop a couple of pounds, while a diet rich in protein can help you gain muscle mass. You can always use a Keto-calculator to determine the right quantity of protein for you.

2. **An increase in energy**

Since a Keto diet will optimize the performance of your mitochondria, your cells can have more energy. Similarly, a Keto diet will generate less reactive oxygen species, thus, improving energy efficiency. In summary, through a Keto diet, you can optimize the performance of your cells, get improved energy levels and consequently, get the most out of life.

3. **A decrease in inflammation**

Unless the reactive oxygen species have caused extensive damage, your body's inflammatory processes do not need to repair the damage frequently. Hence, there are lower inflammation levels in your body.

Also, a side benefit of this lower inflammation reduction in pain, especially if you have chronic inflammation and experience constant pain.

4. An improvement in brain function

Through a combination of low-carbs and Ketones in a Keto diet, you can reduce brain inflammation, activate health-promoting neurotropic factors and boost your overall brain's efficiency. With Ketones, the brain can balance the gamma-aminobutyric acid (GABA) and the glutamate. GABA reduces stimulation in the body (an inhibitory neurotransmitter), while glutamate promotes stimulation (an excitation neurotransmitter). Insufficient GABA and excessive glutamate can cause brain fog and lack of focus.

CHAPTER 4

GETTING STARTED ON KETO AFTER 50

Until you start the Keto diet, you won't realize how much carbs you take, and carb craving is the main reason people give up on Keto after a few days. So, before trying the ketogenic diet, it would be best to try and learn as much as you can about nutrition in general and your own nutritional needs in particular.

Keto is a low-carb and moderate-protein diet but unfortunately, these foods are tasty and we usually eat a lot of them. However, once you understand why you have to give up foods you love so much, which foods contain most carbs and protein, and how you can successfully replace them with other low-carb nutrient-rich foods, adopting the Keto diet becomes much less challenging.

With a little bit of effort, you will easily learn how to prepare balanced meals and even keto-friendly cakes and desserts.

A lot of us usually don't like change and changing your diet seems to be particularly difficult. Besides, if you've been eating a certain way for 50 years, and you now want to make some drastic changes in your eating habits, you will not only need to have a lot of self-discipline but you will also need to be highly motivated. Fortunately, what better motivation do you need than to look great and healthy?

Meal planning for Keto starts with making sure you understand your nutritional requirements. Ideally, a keto diet should consist of 70% fats, 20% protein, and 10% carbs. However, when you first start with this diet, you may not be able to stick to this but at least try to reduce carbs while increasing fats. Depending on what your current diet is like and how self-disciplined and motivated you are, it may take you a couple of weeks to just get used to eating Keto.

To work out how many grams of each of the macros you need, you have to use a macro calculator. Then, look for suitable recipes based on ingredients that are available where you live and that you can afford.

It's important not to force yourself to eat foods you hate. A recent Russian study showed that foods we force ourselves to eat just because they are supposedly healthy, become toxic after ingestion. So, don't force yourself to eat anything you hate. There is a reason our body craves or detests certain foods. Instead, try to interpret the signals your body is sending you and satisfy your craving with healthy food choices.

Once you manage to limit your carbs, eating Keto is easy because there is a long list of Keto-friendly foods - cheese, dressings, fats & oils, nuts & seeds, seafood, eggs, poultry, fruits & vegetables, dairy & plant-based butters, meat.

Foods to avoid are sugary drinks and foods, potatoes, processed foods, legumes, high-carb fruit, snacks, factory-farmed meat, and grains.

Weight management gets more and more challenging as we age, mainly due to a slower metabolism and unhealthy eating habits. However, it doesn't mean you cannot have a great body after 50. On the contrary, as people become more health conscious, they try to stay fit and young-looking for as long as they can.

Can Keto Help After 50?

For Bone Health

Since you don't necessarily need to increase dairy intake after 50, it is better to look for ways to improve bone health. One of the best ways to do this is to focus on a Keto diet that has a drastically reduced amount of toxins. However, Fortunately, Keto is based on the premise of a healthy and varied amount of micronutrients from healthful organic sources. It also helps to have a Keto meal rich in varied micronutrients.

In this light, a Keto diet that is:

- low in toxins

- rich in micronutrients, not just a specific macronutrient such as calcium

- has the right balance of macros

- has low to moderate amounts of protein

will provide a solid foundation for better and optimum health. It will also help with better bone health as it gives leverage for an all-encompassing approach to healthy living and lifestyle.

For Inflammation

Chronic inflammation is a common feature for senior citizens especially for many above 50. With aging, comes pain and irritability.

Conditions such as arthritis are not left out and these put a lot of mental, physical and emotional stress on the victim.

However, the good news is Keto can help reduce and eliminate chronic inflammation. This happens when the body, in Ketosis, reduces the production of inflammatory substances produced by the body, hence helping with mitigating these kinds of health conditions.

Controlling Blood Sugar

There is a link between certain diseases such as Diabetes, Alzheimer's Parkinson's and Dementia and blood sugar. A lot of factors have been shown to greatly affect the outcome of diseases such as Alzheimer's. For example, it has been shown that and excess intake of Carbs is a major risk factor for developing these condition.

However, fortunately, the Ketogenic diet is one which has a highly reduced amount of carbs. Also, healthy dietary fats and cholesterol which is the mainstay of Keto have been shown to reduce the risk for brain-related diseases such as Dementia, Parkinson's and Alzheimer's.

Furthermore, Oxidative stress as mentioned earlier is greatly prevented with the Keto Diet as Ketosis is a protective mechanism against body cell damage arising from oxidative stress.

In essence, overall, the Ketogenic diet can be used to improve insulin response and control blood sugar, in addition to helping with improvement in brain and memory function.

Why A Regular Keto Diet May Not be Recommended for You

While a standard Keto diet might be the Holy Grail amongst 20 and 30-year-olds, the same might not hold well with seniors. This is because our bodies run differently at different age phases and what the body might be able to handle and process easily at a younger age may become a tough job at an older age. This is the main reason older adults need a tailored approach to Keto.

While the basics for a standard Keto diet haven't changed, it supports a sudden reduction in carbs. Our bodies' response to this sudden decrease is harder to handle at 50+ compared to youthful 20. And because we have been wired to eat carbs for a long time, getting into Ketosis becomes a hard thing to do.

This may tell on our bodies as we consequently develop the "Keto flu" - symptoms such as:

Constipation

Sleeplessness

Vomiting

Nausea

Fatigue

Headache

Difficulty tolerating exercise

Dizziness

Again, when the Keto flu happens, it becomes even more difficult adapting to and adjusting as a result of age, even making things harder to succeed. It becomes much more difficult to recover and stay on track or progress with Keto. The consequence is a possible give up or calling it quits. But that shouldn't be so. This is because there's a better, gentler approach to Keto after 50.

A Custom-fit Approach to Keto after 50

Anyone over 50 will have a much tougher time living on foods with higher carbs/sugar and high fats when compared to younger people. As a result, it becomes imperative that seniors rely on Keto foods that are not only nourishing but also disease-fighting and health-supporting.

One of the ways to do this is to incorporate healthy fats and MCT oils in the right amounts from olive oil, avocado, and coconut oil. Also, Keto should be supported with supplementation.

Moderately high carb foods such as potatoes, squash, and roots should be cut out entirely; while foods rich in micronutrients should be included. Less nutrient-dense foods such as unnecessary dressings and dipping sauces may be avoided altogether.

You can limit intake of Dairy as it may practically make no difference, but ensure you add enough low carb veggies such as Kale.

It is important if you're over 50 to avoid consumption of foods with empty calories such as foods with added sugars, diet coke, refined grains, etc. and eat more nutrient-dense foods rich in fats and proteins.

5 Tips on Losing Weight after 50:

1.   **Find out your BMI (Body Mass Index)**
This is about your body fat percentage and your waist circumference and your doctor can do this for you. After 50, your waist circumference may increase even if you don't put on weight. The reason for this is that the hormonal changes you're going through change the way fat is stored in your body. Besides, lower testosterone levels in both men and women at this age cause a decrease in muscle mass.

So even if you don't put on weight, after 50 you are likely to feel and look more "fatty" partly because you've lost muscle and partly because fat is distributed in the "wrong" places.

2.   **Adopt healthy eating habits**

It's safe to diet on Keto in your 50s provided you eat only nutrient-dense foods and cut out most processed foods.

3.   Be physically active

There is not much point in dieting if you are not physically active. If you hate exercising, at least make sure you walk for an hour every day (preferably spread out at different times within the day).

4.   Limit alcohol

Cut back on excess drinking because alcohol may affect your overall health at this age. However, you can take occasional low carb alcoholic drinks.

5.   Practice Intermittent Fasting

You can combine Keto with intermittent fasting.

Tracking Calories

Depending on your daily calorie intake, there could be leftovers for some of the recipes. After you've figured out your calorie intake for the day, measure out the excess food quantity into your portion control containers. As a result, you only need to determine the number of containers to achieve your calorie intake for each day.

Pro tip: Fill a container with a mix and match of the foods within the same category. For instance, if your lunch is keto flatbread, fill half of your container with tomato and the other with mushrooms to make one container. If you want to pack your food properly for the day, learn and understand nutrition labels. Thus, you can measure your food portion rather than taking out your calculators to calculate your portion size all the time.

Tracking Ketosis

It's best to embark on the Keto journey by making sure you understand why you are doing this. If it's just to lose weight, what you need to keep track of during your diet, is the percentage of body fat. You can ask your doctor to measure your body fat for you or you can do this yourself by getting a body fat caliper. You measure your body fat by pinching your skin with the caliper and it shows what your body fat percentage is. However, do not measure your body fat during the menstrual cycle, because while you are menstruating your body retains water and you feel like you've gained weight.

Another way of keeping track of your weight loss by taking photographs of yourself every two or three weeks and compare them to what you looked like before you started the diet.

You can also use Ketosis strips to monitor how successful your weight loss is. You can buy these strips at any pharmacy and from your urine, you'll be able to tell if your body is in ketosis. However, ketones take a few days to accumulate in your urine, so you can only use this method if you've been on the Keto diet for more than five days. Don't worry too much about the color your Keto strip changes to, because as long as it changes color, you'll know you're in ketosis.

However, there is no need to measure the level of ketones if you make sure you take less than 20 grams of carbs a day because, with so few carbs, you are definitely in ketosis.

You can also watch for tell-tale signs of ketosis, one of which is the so-called "Keto breath". When you start with the Keto diet, your breath will change and get a "metallic" smell. If it bothers you, drink plenty of water or chew some sugar-free gums.

Tracking ketosis is important but you should also bear in mind that we are all different and that not all diets suit everyone. Although most people benefit from Keto, watch out for possible side-effects which, although not dangerous, could cause some mild (or not so mild) health problems.

3 Most Common Side-Effects of Ketosis:

1.   Low blood sugar (hypoglycemia)
2.   Hypothalamic-Pituitary-Adrenal axis dysfunction (HPA)
3.   Electrolyte/mineral deficiency

To prevent or deal with possible side-effects, you have to understand what is going on in your body while it tries to adapt to a new diet.

But, before you even start tracking your ketones decide why you are following this diet and what your goals are. Some people may just want to improve their sleep pattern so they sleep peacefully throughout the night. Others may want to improve their mental focus, lower the blood pressure, boost physical performance, or reduce cravings. In other words, if you have a goal, it makes dealing with challenges so much easier.

CHAPTER 5

DEALING WITH THE KETO FLU

We are all different and do not react the same way to certain foods or lifestyles. While some people thrive on the Keto diet and quickly start losing weight, others struggle with headaches, brain fog, and general weakness.

We all know that junk food is unhealthy because it contains a lot of salt; however, by eating this kind of food you usually get plenty of sodium, potassium, and magnesium. On the other hand, foods that you are expected to eat on Keto are natural and contain much less salt.

Besides, while dieting, you are expected to drink more water than you usually do and although this helps you detox, it also flushes out the electrolytes faster than you can replenish them. When this happens, you experience what is known as the Keto flu.

Your body is used to burning carbohydrates for energy and when you drastically reduce your carb intake and force it to start burning fat, the body will be in a shock for a few days until it gets used to a different metabolism. It is during this stage that you are most likely to experience the Keto flu.

The most common symptoms of the Keto flu are headache, fatigue, or nausea although some people may also experience stomach pain, dizziness, irritability, diarrhea or constipation, muscle cramps, lack of concentration, disrupted sleep pattern, sugar cravings, heart palpitations, and low energy levels. Fortunately, as soon as your body becomes keto-adapted and stops craving carbs, the symptoms disappear.

To best way to avoid or cope with these symptoms is to ensure you get the micronutrients you've flushed out back into your system. The easiest and quickest way to do this is by taking supplements.

Fortunately, not everyone experience Keto flu when they embark on the ketogenic diet and even if they do, it is usually only two or three of the symptoms. In most people the symptoms disappear in a week or so, but should they persist for more than ten days you are either not eating a balanced diet or for some reason this way of eating doesn't agree with you. In that case, it's best to consult a qualified nutritionist.

3 Main Causes of the Keto Flu:

1.   Keto-adaptation process

Your body's ability to start burning fat instead of carbs for fuel is called metabolic flexibility. People with lower metabolic flexibility are more likely to experience Keto flu symptoms because their body takes longer to adapt to the new diet.

2.   Lack of electrolytes

When you radically decrease the amount of high-carb processed foods and focus on foods rich in fats, you may experience the flu-like symptoms like headaches, fatigue, aches and pains until your body gets used to the new diet. The best thing to do during the transition is to increase your water intake and work out how to replenish minerals you've lost when you stopped eating carbs. To stay healthy during the transition process, make sure you eat nutrient-rich Keto-friendly foods.

3.   Withdrawal from carbs

We know that processed foods are tasty but can be very addictive. This is why cutting back on junk foods often produces withdrawal symptoms similar to those experienced by drug addicts. Those whose diet is based on processed and sugary foods have most trouble adapting to the Keto diet.

So, don't be alarmed if you experience some, or all, of these symptoms for this is only temporary. Instead, try to stay hydrated, replenish electrolytes, exercise, increase fat intake, adopt a balanced diet, and get plenty of sleep.

CHAPTER 6

STAYING KETO-ADAPTED

There is a difference between ketosis and keto-adaptation.

– **Ketosis is a metabolic state with ketone bodies of 0.5mMols and above**

You can reach ketosis after fasting for 24 hours although it doesn't mean that your body will automatically start burning fat for fuel.

– **Keto adaptation is the process by which your body gradually adapts to using fat as a primary source of energy instead of glucose**

Keto adaptation is a process your body undergoes as it adapts to fewer carbs and proteins and more fat. Once it depletes all the stored glucose reserves, it will have to start burning fat for fuel and this is when you start losing weight quickly.

The goal of all "Ketoers" is to become keto-adapted as soon as possible because once they are, their metabolism changes so the body starts looking for fat when it needs an energy source.

Although you can't lose weight unless you reduce your calorie intake, you will lose it much faster once you are keto-adapted because it is fat, rather than carbs that will be burned.

However, keto-adaptation is not only good for weight-loss; it has many other health benefits.

4 Benefits of Keto-Adaptation:

1.   Your energy levels and blood sugar level remain stable throughout the day and you will no longer have energy crashes.

2.   Ketogenesis and production of ketones are increased and so your brain, heart, and muscles get more fuel.

3.   It helps with mental clarity which means your concentration, memory, and cognitive performance improve.

4.   You are much less likely to experience inflammation and oxidative stress.

5.   Your body is protected from muscle catabolism when you skip meals or when you fast.

6.   You stop craving food throughout the day and this means you'll stop bad snacking, which is a major cause of weight gain.

How to Become Keto-Adapted?

By adopting a ketogenic diet. However, although ketosis for you may mean that you are keto-adapted and are burning fat, there are different degrees of keto-adaptation.

—   If you are on the keto diet but, from time to time, decide to eat a meal rich in carbohydrates, you will kick yourself out of ketosis, reduce your blood ketones, and decrease your body's fat oxidation.

—   If you eat a meal that contains more carbs than allowed on the Keto diet (which may not be a lot of carbs), such a meal is still going to inhibit ketosis.

—   When you abstain from food for about 4-6 hours, you gradually increase the amount of fat being burned however, that doesn't mean you are producing ketones. To start producing ketones, you first have to deplete your liver glycogen by fasting for 16-20 hours, eating Keto for a few days, or exercising for several hours non-stop.

—   You can be in ketosis after 20 hours of fasting but you may experience the Keto flu because your body is not keto-adapted. So, to improve using ketones for fuel and increase keto-adaptation, you have to follow the keto diet for more than a couple of days. The first major improvements in performance happen in 2-3 weeks, 2-3 months or 6-12 months. It all depends what your goals are, how keto-adapted you are, and how strictly you follow the keto lifestyle.

The healthiest way to start producing ketones and burning fat is to gradually become keto-adapted rather than try to reach ketosis overnight by fasting for 24 hours. The only thing you will achieve this way is to put your body under unnecessary stress and experience some of the keto-flu symptoms. When it comes to Keto, easy does it.

CHAPTER 7

FIGHTING DISEASE WITH THE KETO DIET

Most of the diseases of modern civilization, eg cancer, stroke, heart disease, autoimmune disorders, diabetes, obesity, etc are food-related which means they can be managed, avoided, and even reversed by a change of diet. One of the diets that have proven successful with some of the most debilitating diseases is the ketogenic diet.

Keto diet was discovered by accident and was initially used as an alternative treatment for some neurological conditions. However, over the years, it became apparent that it can provide relief with many other conditions.

15 Conditions that can benefit from the Keto Diet:

1.   Epilepsy

Epileptic seizures happen because of increased brain activity and although there is very good drug therapy, not everyone responds to anti-seizure medications. Fortunately, the ketogenic diet provides relief from seizures in about 50% of epilepsy patients. However, you can only monitor its effectiveness by discussing a suitable plan with your doctor or dietician. Also, you should join Keto communities online and in your locality so that you can strictly follow the diet.

2.   Metabolic Syndrome

Metabolic syndrome is characterized by insulin resistance and people most likely to be affected by it are those with high triglycerides, low levels of "good" cholesterol, high blood pressure, and large waistline (e.g. more than 89 cm in women), i.e. the obese. What's more, this syndrome is often a cause of diabetes or heart disease. A ketogenic diet can easily reduce triglycerides, as well as lower the blood pressure and blood sugar levels and indirectly assist with weight loss.

3.   Glycogen Storage Disease

People with glycogen storage disease (GSD) lack one of the enzymes involved in storing glucose (blood sugar). This disease is usually diagnosed in childhood and manifests as poor growth, fatigue, low blood sugar, muscle cramps, and an enlarged liver. Although this is a very complex condition, patients who follow a ketogenic diet can easily get relief from some of the symptoms.

4.   **Polycystic Ovary Syndrome**

Polycystic ovary syndrome (PCOS) is caused by hormonal dysfunction and it often results in irregular periods and infertility. Many women with this condition are obese, have increased risk of type 2 diabetes or find it impossible to lose weight. However, once on a ketogenic diet, they start losing weight, their insulin levels go down, and their reproductive hormones work better.

Over 70% of infertility issues in women can be traced to PCOS. While a Keto diet can be effective for treating PCOS, women have to be particularly careful because this diet can increase cortisol levels and consequently increase insulin resistance. However, some women can start by slowly reducing their overall carbohydrate intake.

5.   **Diabetes**

Ketogenic diet seems to be particularly beneficial for people with both type 1 and type 2 diabetes because it helps them reduce blood sugar levels in a matter of days. There are cases where patients could even stop taking medication. A complete Keto diet has proven to be the best way to control and perhaps treat type 1 diabetes. But before you make any changes to your diet, consult your doctor.

Evidence from researchers has proven that blood sugar levels in type 2 diabetic patients can be better controlled with a low-carb diet than a high-carb diet. They also discovered that you could attain better blood sugar levels and consequently increased insulin sensitivity with lesser carbohydrate consumption.

It has also been helpful to people suffering from:

- Obesity

- High blood sugar levels

- Chronic inflammation

6.   Certain Types of Cancer

Recent research suggests that a ketogenic diet may help with some types of cancer when used in conjunction with chemotherapy, radiation, and surgery. Keto seems to be particularly efficient in the case of brain cancer. If you're undergoing cancer treatment, ask your doctor whether you can be on a Keto diet. Then, use Keto communities (both offline and online) to support you through your recovery process.

7.   Autism

This serious condition is characterized by problems with communication and social interaction. It usually starts in childhood and although there are different therapies that help with this disorder, many patients experience seizures similar to those caused by epilepsy. A ketogenic diet can help those that don't respond well to anti-seizure medication.

8.   Parkinson's Disease

Parkinson's Disease (PD) is a nervous system disorder characterized by low levels of dopamine. This causes tremor, impaired posture, stiffness, and difficulty walking and writing. A balanced ketogenic diet can improve some of the symptoms of Parkinson's disease. Since Keto diets usually increase the body's consumption of essential fatty acids, they become useful in severely decreasing the symptoms of Parkinson's disease. You can consult your doctor on being on a complete Keto diet when you have or are just starting to develop Parkinson's disease.

9.   Obesity

Studies show that very low-carb ketogenic diets are more effective for weight loss than low-fat diets. The main reason for this is that a Ketogenic diet successfully reduces hunger which makes it easier to lose weight despite all the fat you take.

10.   Multiple Sclerosis

Multiple sclerosis (MS) destroys the protective covering of nerves and prevents "communication" between the brain and body. Typical symptoms are numbness and problems with balance, vision, and memory. Although a ketogenic diet does not provide a cure for this neurological disorder, it can slow it down and relieve many of the symptoms.

11. Nonalcoholic Fatty Liver Disease

Nonalcoholic fatty liver disease (NAFLD) is the most common liver disease in the Western world. It is strongly linked to type 2 diabetes, metabolic syndrome, and obesity, and these three disorders can all be treated with the ketogenic diet. Keto is beneficial in case of NAFLD mainly because it helps reduce liver fat.

Furthermore, supplementing your meals with low-carb vegetables such as broccoli, kale, and spinach as well as restricting high carbohydrates can be effective in reversing fatty liver diseases.

12. Alzheimer's Disease

Alzheimer's disease is a form of dementia which shares many symptoms of epilepsy and type 2 diabetes – seizures, the inability of the brain to properly use glucose, and inflammation linked to insulin resistance. Beta-hydroxybutyrate (a Ketone body) has been found useful for improving the memory function of people with Alzheimer. Ketone bodies improve brain health by:

- Preventing neuronal loss

- Preserving neuron function

- Protecting brain cells against multiple injuries

MCT oil and increased production of ketones help patients cope with some of the symptoms.

13. Migraine Headaches

Migraine headaches are characterized by severe pain, sensitivity to light, and nausea. Many patients experience fewer or milder headaches once they adopt a ketogenic diet.

Researchers opined that Keto diets could treat migraines effectively by enhancing mitochondrial brain metabolism and inhibiting neural inflammation. To enhance mitochondrial brain metabolism and inhibit neural inflammation, the Ketone bodies block the high concentrations of glutamate and reduce oxidative stress. For best results, ensure you supplement your Keto diet with MCT oil.

14.   Heart Disease

Research published in the British journal of nutrition proved that very-low-carbohydrate Ketogenic diets (VLCKD - VLCKD are diets with less than 50g carbs) double the average increase in HDL experienced by low-fat dieters. The researchers concluded that there are actually cardiovascular benefits of consuming carbohydrate-restricted diets, more so, very limited carb diets.

15.   High Blood Pressure

Combining a low-fat diet and a blood pressure/weight-loss drug is less effective than limiting carbohydrates. For best results, your daily diet should contain no more than 50 grams of carbs. Again, only your doctor and your dietician can confirm that this is the most suitable for you because they know your medical history.

CHAPTER 8

KETO-FRIENDLY SUPPLEMENTS FOR SENIORS

Our nutritional requirements change as we get older and although it would be best to get the necessary nutrition from a balanced diet, this is not always possible. For example, certain foods may not be available where you live, you may not have time or skills to prepare healthy meals, your occupation may require that you spend a lot of time on the road, etc. **Besides, as we age, our digestion becomes weaker and nutrient absorption becomes dif**ficult which is why those over 50 **should** start **taking supplements even if they haven't experienced any health problems.**

However, regardless of your age, many nutritionists recommend that supplements should be taken whenever you make a major change to your diet because they help your body adjust to a new dietary regimen.

The supplements usually recommended for seniors **are calcium, vitamin D, Omega-3 fatty acids, probiotics, B12, and CoQ10.**

However, the Keto diet comes with some side effects and although not everyone experiences them, some people have a hard time getting used to living without carbs. Taking supplements while on a Keto diet ensures that side effects are avoided or limited.

Keto is a unique diet and the reason some people find it difficult, is that to put you in ketosis, it requires that you limit carbs but increase fat intake. This is not the kind of diet most of us are used to. If all your life you've been burning sugar for energy, getting your body to start burning fat may take time.

When it comes to the ketogenic diet, supplementation is necessary mainly as prevention but also to *help you reach ketosis sooner*.

4 Reasons to Take Supplements on a Keto Diet:

1. **Reduce or avoid keto flu symptoms**

2. **Balance electrolytes**

3. **Get more micronutrients**

4. **Support ketone production**

There are many supplements that can help you avoid the side effects of the ketogenic diet. Depending on how well you're coping with the new dietary regimen, you may decide to take some or all of them.

10 Supplements That Will Help You Avoid Side Effects of Keto and Boost Production of Ketones

1. **Exogenous ketones**

This is an external form of ketones which help you get into ketosis faster and provide immediate additional energy.

2. **MCT oil**

It boosts ketone production and prevents a lack of energy, poor memory, and mood swings.

3. **Collagen Peptides**

Collagen makes up 30% of the total protein in our body, but most of us are collagen-deficient. Collagen keeps our hair and skin healthy and can even heal leaky gut. However, regular collagen can prevent ketosis, so if you decide to take this supplement, you should take the keto-friendly collagen.

4. **Electrolytes**

To balance micronutrients

5. **Fiber**

To boost digestion

6.   Fish oil supplements

The best source of Omega-3 fatty acids

7.   Ketone salts

To treat fatigue, lightheadedness, headaches, and constipation

8.   Magnesium

To help with muscle cramps, fatigue, and headache

9.   Vitamin D

To help with calcium absorption

10.   Prebiotics

To help digestion

Others: Spirulina, Chlorella, Dandelion Root, and Turmeric

So, the main purpose of supplements on Keto is to prevent deficiencies, help with weight loss, and boost your energy which may be low due to the absence of carbs.

What supplements you should take while on Keto depends partly on your overall health but also on who you ask because nutritionists often have slightly different views of what a body needs help with while dieting. Besides, some nutritionists recommend taking certain whole foods as Keto supplements, eg spirulina, chlorella, dandelion root, and turmeric.

Although most supplements are available over the counter, it's best to discuss this with your medical practitioner or a qualified nutritionist. However, if you have a chronic condition or are on medication, you must discuss the Keto diet with your doctor to find out how some of the supplements you plan to take interact with prescription drugs you are on.

You may also wonder if there are supplements you should stay away from while on the keto diet.

6 Supplements to Avoid on the Keto Diet:

1.   Gummy vitamins

These are tasty but are packed with sugar. Instead, take sugar-free supplements in a pill, powder, or drop form.

2.   Cheap multi-vitamins

Most multi-vitamins are synthetic products and if you have a sensitive gut, they can cause nausea. Instead, buy vitamins from reliable sources.

3.   Detox products

These are supposed to encourage bowel movements and ease constipation, however, this is only a short-term solution. Instead, take fiber-rich foods and drink plenty of water.

4.   Caffeine pills

If you crave caffeine, take it as coffee because caffeine pills, if taken incorrectly, can cause heart palpitations, anxiety, and insomnia.

5.   Antioxidants

High doses of antioxidants can be counterproductive. Instead, eat a balanced Keto diet.

6.   Vitamin C

We are told vitamin C boosts our immune system and we should take it daily, however, taking more than 2000 mg of vitamin C can increase the risk of kidney stones. Instead, squeeze some lemon juice in every glass of water you take.

KETO DIET BEST FOOD LIST FOR SENIORS

You should generally avoid carb-rich foods when you are on a Keto diet. For more on this, please refer to our **Free Keto Cheat Sheet. Al**though you should restrict carbs, you can still enjoy berries or other low-glycemic fruits within a Keto-friendly micronutrient range.

When you are on a Keto diet, your meals and general diet should consist of: Fats, Protein, and Vegetables

FATS AND OILS

Oils are one of the best sources of healthy fats on the Keto diet. Rich in oleic acid, olive oil is known for decreasing the risk of heart disease. Extra-virgin olive oil is also rich in oleic acid as well as antioxidants such as phenols. These antioxidants improve artery function, decrease inflammation and further protect your heart's health. Olive oil does not contain any carbs since it's a pure source of fat. You can use it to dress salads and provide healthy mayonnaise. However, it is not stable at high temperatures. Thus, your best option is to add it to already cooked foods or for low heat cooking.

Coconut oil is also another best Keto food rich in healthy fats. One of the properties that make it suitable for a Keto diet is that it contains medium-chain triglycerides (MCTs) which can be digested by the liver at once and used as a rapid source of energy, or converted to Ketones. Coconut oil is effective for increasing Ketone levels in people suffering from disorders of the brain and nervous systems such as Alzheimer's disease. Coconut oil also contains fatty acids with Lauric Acid, the main one. With this high amount of fatty acids, coconut oil can promote a sustained level of Ketosis. Furthermore, Coconut oil is effective for losing belly fat and helping obese adults lose weight. Each of these oils differs in their flavors; hence, you should strive to have each variety in your pantry. These oils include;

MCT Oil

Coconut Butter

Nut Oils

Avocado Oils

Coconut Oil and

Extra-Virgin Oil

DAIRY PRODUCTS

These provide your body with a sufficient dosage of calcium, protein, and healthy fats. All types of cheese are Keto-friendly since they are all high in fat and low in carbs. Do you know that one ounce of cheddar cheese contains 7g protein and 1g carbs? Cheese hasn't been proven to exacerbate heart disease despite being high in saturated fat. Also, cheese contains a fat called *Conjugated Linoleic Acid* which is known to improve healthy body composition and help your body lose fat. Regular consumption of cheese can help aging persons by reducing the loss of muscle mass and strength.

Five ounces' cottage cheese contains 5g carbs and 18g proteins, while the same amount of plain Greek yogurt contains 5g carbs and 11g protein. When consumed without being combined with other foods, both of them promote feelings of fullness and decrease in appetite. However, you can prepare a quick and easy Keto treat by combining the cottage cheese and plain Greek yogurt with chopped nuts, cinnamon, and any sugar-free sweetener.

They include;

FULL-FAT DAIRY

All fat dairy products including butter and cream contain lots of conjugated linoleic acid. This fatty acid is responsible for promoting fat loss.

Butter,

Yogurt,

Cream

CREAM & YOGURT

Heavy Cream

Plain Greek Yogurt

FULL FAT CHEESE

Goat Cheese

Brie

Cream Cheese

Cheddar

Mozzarella

Cottage Cheese

NUT BUTTER

Cashew Butter

Natural Peanut

Almond Butter

NUTS AND SEEDS

When you consume nuts frequently, it can reduce your susceptibility to chronic diseases such as depression, certain cancers and heart diseases. All nuts and seeds differ in their quantity of net carbs. They contain lots of healthy fats and proteins that will help you to overcome hunger before your main meals. These include;

Cashews: 8g net carbs

Pumpkin seeds: 4g net carbs

Sesame seeds: 3g net carbs

Almonds: 3g net carbs

Chia seeds: 1g net carbs

Pecans: 1g net carbs

Flaxseeds: 0g net carbs

Macadamia nuts: 2g net carbs

Pistachios: 5g net carbs

Brazil nuts: 1g net carbs

Walnuts: 2g net carbs

Hemp seeds

Hazelnuts

PROTEIN

MEAT, EGGS AND POULTRY

These are the staples of a Ketogenic diet. Apart from being rich in a lot of minerals, B vitamin, and high-quality proteins, fresh meat and poultry do not contain any carbs.

You need to buy a lot of organic poultry and grass-fed organic beef because animal proteins are one of the key components of the Keto diet. Examples in this group are

MEAT AND MEAT PRODUCTS

Pork

Bison

Grass-Fed Beef

Bacon Lamb

Venison

Pork

Beef

Ground Beef

Smoked Meats

New York Strip Steak

ORGAN MEATS

Kidney

Tongue

Gizzards

Heart

Sweetbreads/pancreas

Liver

POULTRY

Chicken

Turkey

Chicken Thighs and Legs

EGGS

Eggs are one of the most diverse and healthiest foods on earth. One large egg contains less than 6g of protein and 1g of carbs. Also, eggs can help your body maintain a stable blood sugar level and consequently, minimize your calorie intake for at least 18 hours. To protect your eye health, it's important that you eat a whole egg completely. Furthermore, antioxidants such as *Lutein* and *Zeaxanthin* as well as other egg nutrients are found in an egg's yolk. Egg yolks can't raise blood cholesterol levels despite being high in cholesterol. Hence, you can consume them as long as it suits your Keto diet daily macros.

Pastured, organic *whole eggs*

SEAFOOD

Fish, shellfish, salmon, sardines and mackerel are amongst Keto-friendly seafood. You should ensure that you consume a minimum of two seafood servings per week.

They are a healthy source of protein, selenium, and omega-3 fatty acids. They include

FATTY FISH

Mackerel

Herring

Wild-Caught Salmon

Cod

Mussels

Tuna

Mackerel

Sardines and

Wild Salmon amongst others

SHELLFISH

Crab

Shrimp

Clams: 5g

Mussels: 7g

Squid: 3g

Octopus: 4g

Oysters: 4g

VEGETABLES

NON-STARCHY VEGETABLES

Low carb and cruciferous vegetables such as cauliflower, broccoli, and kale belong here. Non-starchy vegetables usually have a maximum of 8g net carbs per cup.

They have a high concentration of antioxidants, minerals, vitamin, and fibers. Examples are

Peppers

Mushrooms

Tomatoes

Broccoli

Greens

Kale

Zucchini

Bell Peppers

Brussels Sprouts

Celery

Cabbage

Finocchio

Cauliflower

Broccoli

Mushrooms

Spinach And

Arugula

Fennel

Bok Choy

Cucumber

Lettuce

Green Peppers

FRUITS

LOW SUGAR FRUITS

Despite containing sugar and carbohydrates, there are some fruits that you can include in your Keto diet. Rather than consuming high sugar fruits such as grapes, papayas, pineapples, bananas, pears, and apples, you can substitute with low sugar fruits such as blueberries and raspberries – especially if you crave for something sweet and don't want to fall out of Ketosis. Bottom line: Stock low-carb fruits like raspberries in your refrigerator, so you find something to binge on, with a particularly sweet tooth

Raspberries and blackberries contain the same quantity of digestible carbs and fiber. They contain lots of antioxidants and so, can prevent disease and reduce inflammation. 3.5 ounce of any berry contains up to 12g net carbs per serving.

Raspberries: 6g net carbs

Strawberries: 6g net carbs

Blueberries: 12g net carbs

Blackberries: 5g net carbs

Strawberries

Avocado

Lemon

Limes

BEVERAGES

You can avoid giving up on your coffee and tea by consuming either unsweetened coffee or unsweetened tea. You can choose from several tasty, sugar-free beverages such as unsweetened green tea, unsweetened coffee and sparkling water. You should experiment with various Keto-friendly flavor combinations to add some extra flavor to your water. For example, add two teaspoons of lemon peel and fresh mint to your drinking water. Occasionally, you can enjoy a mixture of tequila (or vodka) with a low-carb drink. Unsweetened Tea and Coffee Both contain caffeine which may improve your mood, alertness, physical performance and even increase your body metabolism. When you consume lots of coffee and tea, you become less susceptible to diabetes. Bear in mind that you shouldn't consume tea lattes and "light" coffee because they contain high-carb flavors since they are prepared with non-fat milk.

TEA

Unsweetened Tea – no carbs

COFFEE

Unsweetened coffee – no carbs

CACAO

While you're free to consume chocolate, confirm from the label that it contains at least 70 percent cacao. Cocoa Powder and Dark Chocolate are very good sources of antioxidants. Cocoa, blueberries and acai berries provide almost equal amounts of antioxidant activity. Dark chocolate may reduce the risk of heart disease since it contains flavanols. Flavanols can help lower blood pressure and keep the arteries healthy. One ounce of dark chocolate contains 3-10g of net carbs.

They include;

Chocolate (≥70% Cacao) – 1 oz (28g) contains 3g net of carbs

SPICES AND CONDIMENTS

If you're interested in condiments not listed here, always make sure to check the nutritional information on the packaging to ensure it doesn't contain loads of sugar.

DIPPING SAUCES & DRESSINGS

Oil-Based Salad Dressings,

Unsweetened Ketchup,

Mustard,

Olive Oil Mayonnaise

SPICES

Fresh Herbs,
Lemon Juice,
Vinegar,
Pepper And Salt

SNACK FOODS

While whole foods are purely recommended when you are on a Keto diet, some pre-packaged snacks are also Keto-friendly. Examples include;

Low-Carb Crackers,

Nuts

Dried Seaweed

Sugar-Free Jerky

No-Added Sugar Nut Butter

Cello Whisps

Pure Parmesan Cheese Crisps

OTHERS

Shirataki Noodles – Less than 1g carb, mostly water-

Olives – 1 oz contain less than 2g total carbs

FOODS TO AVOID

Although a typical Ketogenic diet is limited to 50 grams of carbs per day, a bespoke Keto for you should be much less than that. Typically, not more than 20g net of carbs per day.

Apart from avoiding high-carb foods, there is often a thin line between foods to avoid and foods to eat when on Ketosis.

Before you know such foods, you must:

- Know the foods that can kick you out of Ketosis and those that are Keto-friendly
- Understand the basic principles that make a Keto food right or wrong

But first,

How do you know you are on the correct Keto diet? You are consistently in Ketosis when your blood Ketone levels are at a minimum of 0.5mmol/L. The food you eat is the main yardstick that determines whether or not you are consistently in nutritional Ketosis.

Unfortunately, most of these foods are unsuitable for a Keto diet:

- Tuber-based food products and tubers such as yams, French fries, potato chips, potatoes, etc.
- Fruits such as apples, bananas, and oranges
- Sugar-sweetened products and sugar derivatives such as maple syrup, agave, honey, sports drinks, soda, table sugar
- Grain-based foods and grains such as cereal, granola, pasta, rice, corn, wheat, etc.

The following foods should be avoided:

BEVERAGES

Beer

Sugary Mixed Drinks

Sports Drinks

Sweetened Teas

Juice or any sweetened beverages

Keto After 50

DIPPING SAUCES

Dipping Sauces

Sugary Salad Dressings

Barbecue Sauce

HIGH SUGAR FRUITS

Pineapple

Bananas,

Grapes

Citrus – oranges, grapefruits, tangerines

BEANS

Kidney Beans

Lentils

Chickpeas

Black Beans

STARCHY VEGGIES

Pumpkin,

Peas

Butternut Squash

Leeks

Eggplant

Spaghetti Squash

Potatoes and Other Starchy Vegetables

GRAINS

Tortillas

Breakfast Cereals

Oats

Rice

Wheat

Other Grains and Grain Products

PASTA

Spaghetti,

Noodles or any other pasta

SWEETENERS

Coconut Sugar

Agave Syrup

Maple Syrup

Candy

Ice Cream

Sugar

Sweets and Other Sugary Foods

HIGH CARB SNACKS

Rolls

Doughnuts

Cookies

Crackers

Whole-Wheat Bread And

White Bread

OTHERS

Avocados

There is only 2g net carb count in one-half of a medium avocado (3.5 oz avocado). Avocados are rich in vitamin and minerals such as potassium. The higher your potassium consumption, the easier you can transition to a Ketogenic diet. Avocados are also proven to increase triglyceride and cholesterol levels.

Olives

Olives function similarly to olive oil and the main active ingredient is the antioxidant, Oleuropein. Oleuropein's anti-inflammatory properties may help prevent damage to the body cells. Some research has shown that consuming olives can decrease blood pressure and prevent bone loss. The size of olives will determine their carb content, but their digestible carb content is very low because half of their carbs are fiber. There are 2g total carbs and 1g fiber in one ounce serving of olives. On average, 1g 7-10 olives can result in a net carb count of 1g.

FOODS TO AVOID ALTOGETHER AFTER 50

BEVERAGES

Just like high-carb foods, you should also avoid high-carb drinks when you are on a Ketogenic diet. It is a proven fact that one of the causes of several health issues (including obesity and diabetes) are sugary beverages.

Bear in mind that you shouldn't consume tea lattes and "light" coffee because they contain high-carb flavors since they are prepared with non-fat milk.

SWEETENERS AND ADDITIVES

Aspartame

Sugar Alcohols

Preservatives

Foods with artificial colors or other diet foods

MEATS

Processed Meats Such As

Hot Dogs,

Packaged Foods

Fast foods or any other processed foods

Sugary sauce-marinated meats

Cold cuts of meat with added sugar (always make sure to read the label)

Chicken Nuggets

Fish Nuggets

FATS AND OILS

Corn Oil

Canola

Safflower Oil

Sunflower Oil

Margarine or any artificial fats

VEGGIES

Raisins

Corn

Sweet Potatoes

NUTS AND SEEDS

Dried Fruit

Sweetened Nut Butter

Chocolate-Covered Nuts

Sweetened Seed Butters

Tips For Success

Getting to live the Keto Lifestyle may seem like a herculean task, and indeed depressing. But with your weight loss goals in mind, extra effort towards commitment should be made. I'm going to end this book with extra tips you can use to achieve success on Keto.

For starters, living on restricted carbs may put some shock on your body when starting out, but you can engage your body to handle and recover faster.

If weight loss is your ultimate goal, then you may want to combine Keto with intermittent fasting.

Since Keto has been proven to reduce hunger, it makes more sense and works great with intermittent fasting. Although Keto reduces hunger, many people sometimes still feel hungry on Keto. When you start out on Keto, you may feel hungry too, but don't worry, one of the best things you can do to limit or stop this is to simply stop eating whenever you feel hungry. This may be somewhat ironic, but as simple as it sounds, it works effectively. But if you feel you can't handle it, it helps to take some Keto fat bombs occasionally. Remember, fat bombs with added sugar are just as bad as junk foods!

Another way is to take more water or lemon infused water anytime you have cravings. You can take varied amounts of ice water also. Salt water also helps. Always keep in mind that occasionally, you may be tempted to cheat, but understanding this and getting prepared for it will make things a whole lot easier for you.

Have a very nice looking water bottle close to you all the time for easy access - and of course, as a reminder! However, while drinking enough water and staying hydrated, make sure you urinate whenever you feel the need to do so. But learn to stop drinking too much especially before you go out or before bed time.

One of the greatest problems with many dietary programs is that they are too complicated and difficult to start. A way to mitigate this is to structure your Keto lifestyle and diet menu into a challenge. Depending on your goals, it could be 21 day, 28 day or 30 day challenge. This makes Keto very easy to follow, track and stick with.

Keto for you as a beginner doesn't need to be complicated with difficult-to-source, too-expensive ingredients or too-elaborate instructions. You may find that getting to start Keto this way quickly kills motivation and enthusiasm. Nothing beats Simplicity in Keto and indeed dieting overall. Do not spend too much on protein in a bid to make it enticing with different variety; all you need is simple sources of protein. Although, getting Almond or coconut flour alternatives can be quite expensive when compared to regular white flour, but if that's the price to pay for being healthy, then so be it!

You also need to track calories, and ensure your daily macros are not been exceeded. Otherwise, you may be setting up yourself for a hard time trying to lose weight.

Many people advocate having a "Cheat day". While it is understandable to do so as a beginner, I recommend limiting it to not more than the first month. A better alternative is to try going overboard your daily macros or calories once or twice a week for the first two months; and thereafter, adjusting accordingly.

Keto is very enjoyable if you make it to be so, but always keep your focus on your specific goals – be it weight loss, health improvement, disease management, etc. Having a constant reminder about this keeps your motivation. So when the distractions come, you're better positioned to decipher and handle it.

It also helps to get involved in online Keto communities, or local groups near you. In fact, find yourself a Keto mate, especially one who is very enthusiastic about Keto, or knows the local farmers markets and how to source grocery items easily

Ensure you include healthy fats in your Keto diet. It's not just enough to consume fats – but rather, very healthy fats especially MCTs. In this regard, Coconut oil and MCT Oil are perfect. Remember, unhealthy fats from other sources can cause more harm than good – and can counteract any good or benefit Keto would have given to your health.

Nuts and Nut butter are also great choices for extra fat sources. But incorporate more seeds rather than nuts if you're well over 50.

Again low sugar fruits such as raspberries and blueberries should be incorporated in limited amounts. You want to strictly keep things low carb over 50. Avoid the temptation to add white carbs into your macros.

Always look at food labels before making purchases. You don't want food items with dangerous and unwanted ingredients especially added sugar

Eat plenty of fiber rich foods too; and remember, diet coke and other soft drinks do not count. Avoid them entirely. Or you can replace them with unsweetened tea and coffee.

It also helps to exercise or work out before a meal rather than after.

Declutter your pantry and refrigerator before starting out on Keto. This will limit cheating to a very large extent and also keep you on track Keto. Replace sugary items, junk foods and easy carbs with Keto-rich food ingredients (Please refer to the shopping list guide).

Buy some sophisticated Kitchen equipment and tools as stated earlier in the guide, that is, if you don't already have them. Cooking with them will make preparing Keto meals easier for you.

Let your family and friends know of your dietary lifestyle and choices, so they don't bug you to eat other foods at events or when you're with them. And I'm sure they'll respect that!

Finally, introduce one tip at a time and measure progress. This would enable you track and follow through and determine possible areas for change if need be. If you introduce too many tips at the same time, it would be difficult to know the best tips that work for you. And again, doing otherwise may hamper your overall success. You don't want to do too many things at the same time that would overwhelm your body. Remember, Keto isn't just a diet but a lifestyle.

EXTRA TIP FOR SUCCESS

You can prepare a week's Keto menu from the breakfast, lunch and dinner recipes provided in this book. Remember, when you are on Keto, you need to snack between meals to keep you in track and moderate hunger. There are lots of Keto-friendly snacks in this book, prepare any of them. Bear in mind that if you snack too much every day, you can gain weight. Use your age, weight loss goal, and activity level to determine and consume the suitable amount of calories per day.

In addition to moderate snacking to limit hunger and stay on track Keto, you should have and stick to a shopping list. When you do, you'll avoid the temptation of binging and eating unhealthy foods. Shop for ingredients you'll need for at least a week and plan your meals ahead of time. As previously mentioned, a daily, healthy Keto diet should contain 5% to 10% carbs, 20% protein, and 70% to 75% fat. Use the guide in this section and the recipes compiled to transition into Keto with ease. One of the best ways to be successful when you're on a Keto diet is by planning your meals. It is a proven fact that when you back your motivation with proper planning, you are more likely to succeed. To provide you with additional conviction, see the next section.

P.S. Refer to our free book: *21 Tips, Tricks and Strategies* to make meal prepping and staying on track Keto, successful for you. This will ensure you get the absolute best out of your meal prepping while staying on track the Keto diet.

Measurement Conversion Chart

For many countries including the USA, Canada and most European countries, the measurement units used in this book should suffice. But for many other countries like the United Kingdom, this measurement conversion chart should come in handy and useful.

Cup	Fluid OZ.	MILLILITER	TABLESPOON	TEASPOON
1 cup	8 oz	237 ml	16 x	48 x
¾ c	6 oz	177 ml	12 x	36 x
½ c	4 oz	118 ml	8 x	24 x
¼ c	2 oz	59 ml	4 x	12 x
1/8 c	1 oz	30 ml	2 x	6 x

BREAKFAST RECIPES

Low Car Bacon Egg Scramble

Prep time: 10 min., cook time: 15 min., total time: 25 min.

Serves: 2

Ingredients:

- 1 cup romaine lettuce leafs
- 2 large eggs
- 1 tbsp. heavy cream, whipped
- 4 medium slices bacon, cooked
- 1 slice cheddar cheese, shredded
- $\frac{1}{4}$ tsp salt
- $\frac{1}{4}$ tsp freshly ground black pepper
- $\frac{1}{4}$ tsp onion powder
- $\frac{1}{4}$ tsp garlic powder

Instructions:

1. Cook the bacon till completely done
2. Briskly beat the eggs, cream, and seasonings; scramble the egg mixture
3. Stir in the cheese
4. Mix the scrambled eggs, cheese and bacon into the lettuce
5. Serve!

Nutritional information:

> *Calories 232*
>
> *Fat 17.7g*
>
> *Carbs. 3.1g*
>
> *Protein 15.2g*

Almond Avocado Mousse

Prep time: 5 min., cook time: 10 min., total time: 15 min.

Serves: 2

Ingredients:

- $\frac{3}{8}$ cup unsweetened almond milk
- $\frac{3}{8}$ cup heavy whipping cream
- 1 tsp EZ-Sweetz
- $\frac{1}{4}$ avocado, de-seeded and de-skinned, cut in half
- 4 eggs
- 5 ice cubes

Instructions:

1. Combine the almond milk, heavy whipping cream, eggs and EZ-Sweetz in your blender
2. Add the halved, de-skinned and deseeded avocado and the ice cubes
3. Blend to a smooth consistency
4. Refrigerate till slightly cold (about 10 minutes); serve

Nutritional information:

Calories 262

Fat 22.6g

Carbs. 3.9g

Protein 12.2g

Egg with Avocado

Prep time: 8 min., cook time: 7 min., total time: 15 min.

Serves: 2

Ingredients:

- 7 hard-boiled eggs, peeled and thinly sliced
- 1 avocado, thinly sliced
- 1 tbsp. Lemon juice
- 1 tbsp. Red onion, finely chopped
- 1 tsp fresh dill
- $\frac{1}{4}$ tsp salt
- $\frac{1}{4}$ tsp freshly ground black pepper

Instructions:

1. Stir the avocado and the eggs
2. Add the lemon juice; stir in the pepper, salt, dill, and onion
3. Serve!

Nutritional Information:

Calories 431

Fat 35g

Carbs. 10.9g

Protein 21.5g

Delicious Cheesy Eggs

Prep time: 15 min., cook time: 20 min., total time: 35 min.

Serves: 7

Ingredients:

- $\frac{1}{2}$ onion, chopped
- 1 pepper, sliced
- 2 lbs. lean meat, thickly sliced
- 5 eggs
- 2 tbsp. Heavy cream, whipped
- 3 oz. Cheddar cheese
- 1 tsp kosher salt
- 1 tsp freshly ground black pepper
- 1 tsp onion powder
- 1 tsp garlic powder

Instructions:

1. Set aside translucently fried peppers and onions
2. Cook meat for 6 minutes (3 minutes per side) over high heat
3. Before the meat is cooled; prepare the eggs
4. In a bowl, mix the spices, cream, and eggs. Cook mixture with a non-stick pan till solid; whisk once. Add cheese, whisk again. Pour all mixture in a serving dish. Enjoy!

Nutritional information:

Calories 285

Fat 15.4g

Carbs. 1.8g

Protein 32.9g

Low-Carb Asian Scramble

Prep time: 5 min., cook time: 25 min., total time: 30 min.

Serves: 2

Ingredients:

- 6 oz. Flank steak
- 1 oz. Cubetti pancetta
- 2 oz. Cheddar cheese
- 2 eggs
- 1 tsp salt
- 1 tsp freshly ground pepper

Instructions:

1. Pan-fry each side of the flank steak for 2 minutes each; set aside and slice when it's cool
2. Wash and quarter the ends of the radishes
3. Pan fry the pancetta in a cast iron skillet. Add sliced flank steak into the pan
4. Break the eggs into the batter; add the cheese, salt, and pepper to taste. Cook for 2 minutes
5. Put in the oven and cook for 10 minutes; broil till the eggs are at your desired level (5 minutes)

Nutritional Information:

Calories 444

Fat 29g

Carbs. 3.5g

Protein 41.2g

Breakfast Shell Boost

Prep time: 15 min., cook time: 10 min., total time: 25 min.

Serves: 3

Ingredients:

- 1 cup cheddar cheese, thickly sliced
- $\frac{1}{2}$ tsp cumin
- $\frac{1}{4}$ tsp chili powder

Instructions:

1. Layer sliced cheese in circles on a paper-lined baking sheet
2. Drizzle the cumin and chili powder
3. Bake till edges are almost brown (about 7 minutes)
4. When time is up, remove from oven and allow to cool for one minute
5. Hang the baked cheese circles over wooden spoons placed horizontally on turned upside down glasses. Wait for 5 minutes for them to solidify

Nutritional Information:

Calories 154

Fat 12.6g

Carbs. 0.8g

Protein 9.5g

Meaty Egg Muffins

Prep time: 15 min., cook time: 15 min., total time: 30 min.

Serves: 7

Ingredients:

- $\frac{1}{2}$ oz. Ham steak, quartered
- 1 bunch medium green onions (6 green onions), minced
- 1 can tomatoes, drained, 14.5 oz.
- 6 eggs
- 5 tbsp. Heavy cream
- 1 tsp kosher salt
- 1 tsp freshly ground pepper
- 1 tsp onion powder
- 1 tsp garlic powder
- 5 slices cheddar cheese

Instructions:

1. Mix the spices, heavy cream and eggs
2. Oil-coat your muffin pan and fill each cavity with the egg mixture
3. Cook for 5 minutes at 350 degrees F
4. Switch off the oven, add the vegetables and cook for 10 more minutes
5. Add the cheese and cook for 2 more minutes

Nutritional information: Calories 190, fat 14.9g, carbs. 3g, protein 11.4g

Power Protein Blast

Prep time: 5 min., cook time: 5 min., total time: 10 min.

Serves: 2

Ingredients:

- 3 eggs
- 2 tbsp. heavy whipping cream
- $\frac{1}{2}$ tbsp. garlic powder
- $1\frac{1}{2}$ oz. Cheddar cheese
- $\frac{1}{2}$ tsp kosher salt
- $\frac{1}{2}$ tsp freshly ground pepper

Instructions:

1. Mix the eggs, heavy cream, garlic and cheese in the Vitamix container
2. Blend with the high setting for 5 minutes or till the egg is a bit solid
3. Top with salt and pepper. Then, serve

Nutritional Information:

Calories 240,

Fat 19.2g,

Carbs. 3.1g,

Protein 14.3g

Peanut Butter Sandwich

Prep time: 5 min., cook time: 3 min., total time: 8 min.

Serves: 4

Ingredients:

- 4 egg, large
- 2 tbsp. Almond flour
- $\frac{1}{2}$ tbsp. Coconut flour
- 1 tbsp. Butter
- $\frac{1}{4}$ tsp baking powder
- $\frac{1}{4}$ tbsp. Peanut butter
- $\frac{1}{4}$ tbsp. Jelly

Instructions:

1. Mix all the ingredients (except the peanut butter and jelly) in a container; stir thoroughly to a smooth consistency
2. Microwave the mixture using the [high] setting for 3 minutes
3. Transfer to a flat surface and cut into 4 pieces
4. Garnish with the peanut butter and jelly

Nutritional Information:

    Calories 123

    Fat 9.5g

    Carbs. 2.9g

    Protein 6.7g

Delicious Creamy Protein Scramble

Prep time: 10 min., cook time: 20 min., total time: 30 min.

Serves: 2

Ingredients:

- $\frac{1}{2}$ hollandaise sauce
- 1 large egg
- 2 slices bacon, thickly cut
- 1 slice cheddar cheese
- 1 oz. Almond, dry roasted with salt added
- $\frac{1}{2}$ tbsp. White vinegar

Instructions:

1. Add the vinegar to warm water
2. Weave bacon and cook till crisp
3. Crack the egg into a prep bowl
4. Cook egg yolk and a small quantity of water for 5 minutes
5. Meanwhile, top the almond bun with the bacon weave, cheddar cheese, and cooked egg
6. Garnish with the hollandaise sauce

Nutritional information:

Calories 287

Fat 23.1g

Carbs. 4.2g

Protein 17.1g

LUNCH RECIPES

Spicy Baked Cheesy Lunch

Prep time: 7 min., cook time: 5 min., total time: 15 min.

Serves: 4

Ingredients:

- 4 oz. Parmesan cheese, thinly sliced
- $\frac{1}{4}$ tsp paprika
- $\frac{1}{2}$ tsp black pepper (ground)
- $\frac{1}{2}$ tsp Italian seasoning
- $\frac{1}{4}$ tsp salt
- $\frac{1}{2}$ tsp garlic powder
- $\frac{1}{2}$ medium jalapeno peppers, de-seeded and chopped

Instructions:

1. Put 1 tbsp. Cheese on a paper-lined baking sheet
2. Mix the seasonings; sprinkle on the cheese
3. Bake the seasoned cheese mixtures at 400 degrees f. For 5 minutes or till edges are golden brown
4. Drain excess fats by transferring the baked cheese chips to a paper towel. Serve!

Nutritional Information:

    Calories 95

    Fat 6.2g

    Carbs. 1.7g

    Protein 9.1g

Beefy   Veggie Wrap

Prep time: 20 min., cook time: 15 min., total time: 35 min.

Serves: 2

Ingredients:

- $\frac{1}{4}$ lb. Grass-fed lamb, lean
- $\frac{1}{4}$ cup parsley
- $\frac{1}{4}$ tbsp. fresh turmeric, chopped
- $\frac{1}{2}$ tsp kosher salt

Instructions:

1. Soak wooden kebab skewers in water for 40 minutes
2. Pulse parsley till finely chopped (about 1 minute)
3. Add the lamb, and chopped turmeric, pulse to a smooth consistency
4. Tightly wrap the lamb around the wooden kebab skewers; add salt
5. Grill kebabs for 20 minutes
6. Remove from the oven; serve!

Nutritional Information:

Calories 128

Fat 5.7g

Carbs. 1g

Protein 17.3g

Preppy Bacon Cakes

Prep time: 7 min., cook time: 5 min., total time: 12 min.

Serves: 4

Ingredients:

- $\frac{1}{4}$ lb. Bacon, sliced
- $\frac{1}{2}$ tsp. Baking powder
- $\frac{1}{2}$ medium jalapeno pepper
- $\frac{1}{4}$ tsp salt
- 1 egg
- 1 tbsp. Cream cheese
- 1 tsp butter
- 1 tbsp. Golden flaxseed meal
- 2 tbsp. Almond flour

Instructions:

1. Cook sliced bacon till crisp using medium heat
2. Set aside the crisp bacon
3. Mix the remaining ingredients in a large bowl (use $\frac{1}{4}$ medium jalapeno pepper)
4. Split the batter equally in mugs
5. Layer in mugs and microwave for 2 minutes
6. Take out the mug cake from the mugs

Nutritional Information:

 Calories 167

 Fat 13.2g

 Carbs. 1.4g

 Protein 10.3g

Almond Bread

Prep time: 2 min., cook time: 5 min., total time: 7 min.

Serves: 3

Ingredients:

- $\frac{1}{2}$ cup almond flour
- 1 tsp baking powder
- 2 large eggs

Instructions:

1. Pulse all the ingredients to smooth consistency
2. Microwave mixture till fully cooked (about 5 minutes)
3. Separate the bread from the mug
4. Allow to warm, slice, toast and serve!

Nutritional Information:

Calories 77

Fat 5.5g

Carbs. 2g

Protein 5.2g

Spicy Veggie Beef Salad

Prep time: 15 min., cook time: 10 min. total time: 25 min.

Serves: 2

Ingredients:

- 3 oz. ground beef
- $\frac{1}{4}$ tsp salt
- $\frac{1}{4}$ tsp freshly ground black pepper
- $\frac{1}{2}$ tsp paprika
- $\frac{1}{2}$ tbsp. butter
- $\frac{1}{2}$ tbsp. olive oil
- $\frac{1}{2}$ large lettuce leaf
- $\frac{1}{2}$ slice cheese
- $\frac{1}{2}$ tsp mayonnaise

Instructions:

1. Flavor the beef with paprika, salt and pepper, then, mix thoroughly
2. Form 2 flat patties; line the center of one patty with butter
3. Merge the second patty with the buttered patty
4. Heat olive oil in a small skillet over high heat and cook each side of the patty for 4 minutes
5. Once the edges are crispy, put the patty on a lettuce leaf, spread the cheese and mayo on it; fold and serve!

Nutritional Information:

Calories 173

Fat 11.8g

Carbs. 1.9g

Protein 15g

Cheesy Jar Salad

Prep time: 10 min., cook time: 4 min., total time: 13 min.

Serves: 4

Ingredients:

- $\frac{1}{4}$ cup fresh basil, chopped
- 3 tbsp. Olive oil
- 1 fresh tomato
- 4 oz. Fresh mozzarella, sliced
- $\frac{1}{4}$ tsp kosher salt

Instructions:

1. Create a basil paste by pulsing the chopped basil with 2 tbsp. Olive oil
2. Slice the tomato (into 4 pieces) and the mozzarella
3. Layer the sliced tomato and mozzarella on the basil paste; season with pepper, salt, and the remaining olive oil
4. Bake in the oven at 400 degrees F for one minute

Nutritional Information:

Calories 346

Fat 31.1g

Carbs. 3.3g

Protein 16.4g

So Good Mushroom Pizza

Prep time: 10 min., cook time: 15 min., total time: 25 min.

Serves: 4

Ingredients:

- 3 large mushroom
- 5 tsp. Olive oil
- $\frac{1}{4}$ tsp salt
- $\frac{1}{4}$ tsp pepper
- 1 medium vine tomato, thinly sliced
- $\frac{1}{4}$ cup fresh chopped basil
- 15 slices pepperoni
- 4 oz. Fresh mozzarella cheese

Instructions:

1. Remove the core of the mushroom to about 1cm thickness
2. Coat the inner part of each mushroom with 1 tsp olive oil (3 tsp olive oil for all the mushrooms); season with salt and pepper
3. Broil mushroom for 5 minutes
4. Repeat the same for the other side of the mushroom
5. Layer the tomato and the basil into each mushroom (about 1 tsp basil and3 tomato slices for each mushroom)
6. Layer 5 pepperoni slices into each mushroom, top each mushroom with 1 oz. Cheese
7. Broil once more for four additional minutes till cheese melts and starts browning

Nutritional information:

Calories 240

Fat 20g

Carbs. 2.6g

Protein 13.4g

Sumptuous Bacon Wraps

Prep time: 15 min., cook time: 30 min., total time: 45 min.

Serves: 3

Ingredients:

- 8 medium jalapeno peppers
- $\frac{1}{4}$ tsp salt
- $\frac{1}{4}$ tsp pepper
- $\frac{1}{4}$ cup mozzarella cheese
- 4 oz. Cream cheese
- 8 medium slices bacon

Instructions:

1. Preheat oven to 425 degrees F
2. Remove the stems of your pepper, cut each into half and remove the core
3. Apart from the bacon, mix the other ingredients in a bowl
4. Insert the cream mixture between two halves of the pepper; press firmly to look like they were never split
5. Wrap each pepper with bacon slices
6. Bake wrapped pepper for 30 minutes

Nutritional Information:

Calories 429

Fat 35.3g

Carbs. 4.7g

Protein 22.9g

Nutty Cheesy Salad

Prep time: 5 min., cook time: 7 min., total time: 7 min,

Serves: 4

Ingredients:

- 2 medium slices bacon, cooked
- 2 oz. Mixed greens
- 2 tbsp. Shaved parmesan
- 3 tbsp. Roasted pine nuts
- $\frac{1}{4}$ tsp salt
- $\frac{1}{4}$ tsp freshly ground pepper

Instructions:

1. Cook bacon till crunchy
2. Layer the greens in a container you can shake without spilling the content
3. Crumble the bacon and the remaining ingredients in the container; shake vigorously to coat all contents evenly

Nutritional Information:

Calories 142

Fat 9.5g

Carbs. 4.2g

Protein 9.9g

Low-Carb Power Meatballs

Prep time: 7 min., cook time: 18 min., total time: 25 min.

Serves: 3

Ingredients:

- $\frac{1}{2}$ lb. Lean ground beef
- $\frac{1}{2}$ tsp garlic powder
- $\frac{1}{2}$ tsp onion powder
- 1 tbsp. Parsley
- $\frac{1}{3}$ tsp freshly ground black pepper
- $\frac{1}{2}$ tsp sea salt

Instructions:

1. Combine all the ingredients
2. Roll the mixture on a paper-lined baking sheet
3. Create 5 meatballs from the mixture; layer meatballs on a baking sheet
4. Bake balls at 400 degrees F for 18 minutes

Nutritional Information:

Calories 144

Fat 4.7g

Carbs. 0.9g

Protein 23.1g

Easy Baked Chili Lunch

Prep time: 15 min., cook time: 10 min., total time: 25 min.

Serves: 3

Ingredients:

- 1 cup cheddar cheese, thickly sliced
- $\frac{1}{2}$ tsp cumin
- $\frac{1}{4}$ tsp chili powder

Instructions:

6. Layer sliced cheese in circles on a paper-lined baking sheet
7. Drizzle the cumin and chili powder
8. Bake till edges are almost brown (about 7 minutes)
9. When time is up, remove from oven and allow to cool for one minute
10. Hang the baked cheese circles over wooden spoons placed horizontally on turned upside down glasses
11. Wait for 5 minutes for them to solidify

Nutritional Information:

Calories 154

Fat 12.6g

Carbs. 0.8g

Protein 9.5g

DINNER RECIPES

Spicy Meatza and Cheese

Prep time: 15 min., cook time: 10 min. total time: 25 min.

Serves: 2

Ingredients:

- 3 oz. ground beef
- $\frac{1}{4}$ tsp salt
- $\frac{1}{4}$ tsp freshly ground black pepper
- $\frac{1}{2}$ tsp paprika
- $\frac{1}{2}$ tbsp. butter
- $\frac{1}{2}$ tbsp. olive oil
- $\frac{1}{2}$ large lettuce leaf
- $\frac{1}{2}$ slice cheese

Instructions:

6. Flavor the beef with paprika, salt and pepper, then, mix thoroughly
7. Form 2 flat patties; line the center of one patty with butter
8. Merge the second patty with the buttered patty
9. Heat olive oil in a small skillet over high heat and cook each side of the patty for 4 minutes
10. Once the edges are crispy, put the patty on a lettuce leaf, spread the cheese on it; fold and serve!

Nutritional Information:

Calories 173

Fat 11.8g

Carbs. 1.9g

Protein 15g

Meaty Curry Dish

Prep time: 10 min., cook time: 15 min., total time: 25 min.

Serves: 4

Ingredients:

- 2 tbsp. Coconut oil
- $\frac{1}{2}$ small onion, chopped
- 1 garlic clove
- 1 tbsp. Curry powder
- $\frac{1}{4}$ lb. Lean ground beef
- 2 tbsp. Coconut cream
- 3 cups spinach, finely chopped

Instructions:

1. Fry sliced onion in hot coconut oil over medium heat till onions are translucent
2. Stir in the curry powder and garlic; cook for one more minute
3. Stir in the beef and cook till doneness. Stir in the coconut cream
4. Add a handful of the chopped spinach in the simmering curried beef
5. Stir till the spinach is wilted; repeat with the remaining spinach
6. Transfer to serving dish, top with coconut cream and serve

Nutritional Information:

Calories 143

Fat 10.7g

Carbs. 3.2g

Protein 9.8g

Chicken Egg Soup

Prep time: 5 min., cook time: 5 min., total time: 10 min.

Serves: 4

Ingredients:

- 2 cups chicken broth
- 1 tbsp. Chicken bouillon, 1/2 cubed
- 1 tbsp. Butter
- 1 tbsp. Garlic paste
- 2 eggs, large

Instructions:

1. Heat a pan using medium-high heat
2. Stir it in the chicken broth, bouillon cube, and butter
3. Boil, stir, add the garlic paste, stir again and switch off the heat
4. Stir beaten eggs in the steaming broth; simmer for 5 minutes

Nutritional Information:

    Calories 306

    Fat 23.1g

    Carbs. 3.6g

    Protein 21g

Healthy Pork Chops

Prep time: 5 min., cook time: 10 min., total time: 15 min.

Serves: 3

Ingredients:

- 4 oz. bone-in pork chops
- $\frac{1}{4}$ cup coconut flour
- $\frac{1}{2}$ tsp seasoned salt
- $\frac{1}{2}$ tsp freshly ground black pepper
- $\frac{1}{2}$ tbsp. Butter

Instructions:

1. Mix all the dry ingredients in a large mixing bowl
2. Dry the pork chops. Drizzle dry ingredients over pork chops
3. Swirl butter in a hot pan over high heat
4. Fry pork chops in the melted butter (5 minutes per side)

Nutritional Information:

Calories 299

Fat 14.4g

Carbs. 6.9g

Protein 33.6g

Veggie Steaks

Prep time: 10 min., cook time: 20 min., total time: 30 min.

Serves: 2

Ingredients:

- 1 tbsp. Butter
- 2 button mushrooms, thinly sliced
- $\frac{1}{2}$ small onion, thinly sliced and cut in half
- 1 bell pepper, cut in $\frac{1}{4}$-inch slices
- $\frac{1}{4}$ serving ribeye steak, seasoned
- $\frac{1}{2}$ tsp salt
- $\frac{1}{2}$ tsp freshly ground black pepper

Instructions:

1. Season the rib eye with the salt and pepper
2. Cook a mixture of mushroom, bell pepper and onions in melted butter for 7 minutes
3. Separate the veggies into the sides of the pan; layer the seasoned rib eye steak at the center
4. Add 1 tbsp. butter, cook for 5 more minutes. Serve at once!

Nutritional Information:

Calories 352

Fat 24.7g

Carbs. 8.8g

Protein 24.9g

Spicy Protein Balls

Prep time: 10 min., cook time: 20 min., total time: 30 min.

Serves: 2

Ingredients:

- $\frac{1}{2}$ lb. Ground Pork
- $\frac{1}{2}$ tsp garlic powder
- $\frac{1}{4}$ tsp kosher salt
- $\frac{1}{8}$ tsp freshly ground pepper
- $\frac{1}{4}$ tsp dried sage
- $\frac{1}{4}$ tsp dried thyme

Instructions:

1. Evenly distribute the ingredients on the ground pork
2. Create balls from the mixture
3. Flatten the balls into equal patty shapes
4. Cook the sausage patty in hot oil over medium heat till patties are golden brown

Nutritional Information:

Calories 165

Fat 4g

Carbs. 0.7g

Protein 29.8g

Low Carb Chicken "Zoodles"

Prep time: 10 min., cook time: 20 min., total time: 30 min.

Serves: 3

Ingredients:

- 1 lb. Chicken breast, cubed
- 1 cup heavy cream, whipped
- $\frac{1}{2}$ cup chicken broth
- 1 tbsp. Italian seasoning
- 1 tbsp. garlic seasoning
- 2 zucchinis, noodled
- $\frac{1}{2}$ cup cherry tomatoes
- $\frac{1}{2}$ cup spinach

Instructions:

1. Cook the chicken and set aside
2. Cook a mixture of the grated cheese, chicken broth, and heavy cream over medium heat; frequently stir to thicken the mixture
3. Add $\frac{1}{4}$ cup each of the cherry tomatoes and spinach
4. Cook till spinach wilts (approximately five minutes)
5. Add the zucchini noodles; cook for three more minutes. Serve at once!

Nutritional Information:

Calories 276

Fat 15.4g

Carbs. 7.2g

Protein 27.1g

Cheesy Fish Fusion

Prep time: 10 min., cook time: 25 min., total time: 35 min.

Serves: 4

Ingredients:

- 3 salmon fillets, skin removed
- 2 oz. asparagus spears, trimmed wood ends
- juice of $\frac{1}{2}$ a lemon
- 2 tbsp. garlic, ground
- 3 tsp dried parsley, minced
- $\frac{1}{8}$ tsp salt
- $\frac{1}{8}$ tsp freshly ground black pepper
- $\frac{1}{2}$ oz. fresh grated parmesan cheese

Toppings:

- 1 lemon wedge
- 2 tsp parsley, ground

Instructions:

1. Arrange the salmon fillets centrally in a large aluminum foil. Split the asparagus into 4 equal parts; layer each part with the salmon
2. In a separate bowl, mix the melted butter, lemon juice, garlic and parsley. Drizzle this mixture over each salmon and asparagus pair
3. Add salt and pepper to desired taste; add 3 tablespoon parmesan cheese
4. Seal edges to prevent butter leakage
5. Bake at 450 degrees f. For 10 minutes
6. (if you desire a crispy top, broil for 2 minutes till cheese is golden)
7. Top with the extra parsley and lemon wedges

Nutritional Information:

> Calories 206
>
> Fat 9.1g
>
> Carbs. 4.8g
>
> Protein 28g

Low-Carb Garnished Parmesan

Prep time: 7 min., cook time: 10 min., total time: 17 min.

Serves: 3

Ingredients:

- 3 oz. Parmesan, minced
- $\frac{1}{4}$ tsp chili powder
- $\frac{1}{4}$ tsp freshly ground black pepper
- 1 small tomato, chopped

Instructions:

1. Mix the first three ingredients
2. Gently spread 1 tbsp. Of this mixture on a baking sheet
3. Repeat for all the parmesan
4. Bake parmesan till crispy (about 5 minutes)
5. Spray the chopped tomato on the chips; bake for 2 additional minutes
6. Remove from oven, serve after 5 minutes

Nutritional Information:

Calories 145

Fat 9.2g

Carbs. 3.6g

Protein 14g

Lemoned Broccoli Casserole

Prep time: 5 min., cook time: 25 min., total time: 30 min.

Serves: 3

Ingredients:

- $\frac{1}{4}$ lb. Broccoli florets
- 4 oz. Parmesan cheese
- 1 tbsp. Fresh basil, ground
- 1 tsp garlic, finely chopped
- $\frac{1}{2}$ tsp kosher salt
- $\frac{1}{2}$ tsp red chili flakes
- Zest of $\frac{1}{4}$ lemon
- Juice of $\frac{1}{4}$ lemon

Instructions:

1. Arrange broccoli florets on a paper-lined baking sheet
2. Season broccoli with the lemon zest, lemon juice, red chili flakes, salt, garlic, and basil
3. Top with the parmesan cheese and bake for 25 minutes
4. Transfer to a serving dish

Nutritional Information:

Calories 146

Fat 8.7g

Carbs. 4.9g

Protein 14.1g

SNACK RECIPES

Keto Pesto Pizza

Prep time: 15 min., cook time: 0 min., total time: 15 min.

Serves: 2

Ingredients:

- 2 oz. Cream cheese
- 7 slices pepperoni
- 4 black olives, cavity removed
- 1 tbsp. Tomato pesto, sun-dried
- 1 tbsp. Fresh basil, shredded
- $\frac{1}{4}$ tsp kosher salt
- $\frac{1}{4}$ tsp freshly ground black pepper

Instructions:

1. Thinly slice the olives and the pepperoni
2. Combine the cream cheese, pesto, tomato and basil
3. Stir in the thinly sliced pepperoni and olives into the mixture
4. Create balls from the mixture; top with spices. Serve with sauce (optional)

Nutritional Information:

> *Calories 221*
>
> *Fat 19.7g*
>
> *Carbs. 2.6g*
>
> *Protein 8.5g*

Cacao-Ower Energy Balls

Prep time: 10 min., freeze time: 20 min., total time: 30 min.

Serves: 3

Ingredients:

- $\frac{1}{4}$ cup coconut oil
- $\frac{1}{8}$ cup cocoa powder
- 3 tbsp. Hemp seeds; shelled
- 1 tbsp. Heavy cream
- 2 tsp vanilla extract
- 15 drops liquid stevia
- $\frac{1}{8}$ cup coconut flakes, unsweetened

Instructions:

1. Form a paste from a mixture of all the ingredients, except the coconut flakes
2. Create balls with the mixture
3. Completely dip the balls into the coconut flakes
4. Arrange each ball on a paper-lined parchment paper; freeze (about 20 minutes)

Nutritional Information:

    Calories 297

    Fat 29.9g

    Carbs. 3g

    Protein 6g

Blueberry Brain Booster

Prep time: 5 min., cook time: 0 min., total time: 5 min.

Serves: 1

Ingredients:

- 5 ice cubes
- $\frac{1}{5}$ cup coconut milk, unsweetened
- $\frac{1}{2}$ tbsp. Sour cream
- $\frac{1}{2}$ tbsp. Golden flaxseed meal
- $\frac{1}{4}$ tbsp. MCT oil
- 10 drops liquid stevia
- $\frac{1}{2}$ tbsp. Blueberry extract
- $\frac{1}{5}$ tbsp. Banana extract
- 3 small eggs

Instructions:

1. Pulse all the ingredients together at high setting till mixture is smooth and thick
2. Refrigerate to cool; serve cold

Nutritional Information:

    Calories 402

    Fat 30.4g

    Carbs. 11.7g

    Protein 20.8g

Keto Avocado Smoothie

Prep time: 5 min., cook time: 0 min, total time: 5 min.

Serves: 2

Ingredients:

- 1 oz. Coconut Milk Full Fat
- 4 oz. water
- $\frac{1}{2}$ cup Cauliflower raw
- $\frac{1}{2}$ avocado
- 2 scoop collagen protein
- 1 tsp vanilla extract
- 1 tbsp. spearmint, fresh
- 1 tbsp. cacao powder
- 1 tbsp. coconut oil
- $\frac{1}{5}$ bar ceylon cinnamon
- $\frac{1}{4}$ tsp Himalayan sea salt

Instructions:

1. Blend all the ingredients till they form a smooth mixture
2. Refrigerate to cool
3. Serve!

Nutritional Information:

Calories 289

Fat 21.4g

Carbs. 9.9g

Protein 17.7g

Nutty Cacao Balls

Prep time: 5 min., cook time: 10 min., total time: 15 min.

Serves: 3

Ingredients:

- $\frac{1}{3}$ cup mascarpone cheese, minced
- $\frac{1}{2}$ tsp vanilla extract
- 1 tbsp. cacao powder (optional)
- 2 tsp erythritol
- $\frac{3}{5}$ cup pistachios, chopped
- 5 oz. cheddar cheese

Instructions:

1. Mix the minced cheese, vanilla, and Erythritol in a small bowl
2. Blend the mixture to complete smoothness
3. Form 5 balls with the mixture
4. Roll each ball in the pistachios till they are well coated
5. Microwave for 15 minutes
6. Serve!

Nutritional Information:

Calories 304

Fat 24.9g

Carbs. 8.1g

Protein 17.3g

Baked Bread Bites

Prep time: 10 min., cook time: 10 min., total time: 20 min. *Serves*: 7

Ingredients:

- 2 oz. parmesan cheese, ground
- 2 tsp baking powder
- 2 oz. cream cheese, softened
- 2 large egg, beaten
- 4 tbsp. onions, minced
- 4 olives pimientos, drained
- $\frac{2}{3}$ cup cheddar cheese, thinly sliced
- $\frac{1}{2}$ cup avocado oil

Instructions:

1. Combine the parmesan and baking powder in a mixing bowl
2. Stir in the cheddar, pimientos, beaten egg, onions and cream cheese
3. If balls can't be formed from the dough, add more parmesan to thicken it
4. Heat $\frac{1}{2}$ cup of fat at 400 degrees F over medium heat
5. Form balls with two tablespoon of the dough; gently place balls in the hot fat
6. Fry for 5 minutes or till edges are light brown
7. Transfer fried balls to serving platter; repeat to exhaust the remaining dough
8. Garnish with pimiento mayo. Refrigerate extra balls for up to 72 hours

Nutritional Information:

Calories 157

Fat 13g

Carbs. 2.9g

Protein 7.9g

Chocolate Nut Power Bars

Prep time: 10 min., cook time: 5 min., total time: 15 min.

Serves: 4

Ingredients:

- $\frac{1}{2}$ cup chocolate chips
- $\frac{1}{4}$ cup almond butter
- $\frac{1}{8}$ cup sticky sweetener
- $\frac{1}{8}$ cup coconut oil
- 1 cup nuts and seeds

Instructions:

1. Set aside a parchment paper-lined baking sheet
2. Melt a mixture of the chocolate chips, almond butter, sticky sweetener and coconut oil to smooth consistency
3. Stir in your nuts and seeds.
4. When fully combined, pour mixture into the lined baking dish and spread with a food turner
5. Freeze till solid

Nutritional Information:

Calories 322

Fat 25.3g

Carbs. 10.6g

Protein 14.1g

Awesome No-Sugar Dessert

Prep time: 10 min., cook time: 0 min., total time: 10 min.

Serves: 2

Ingredients:

- 1 cup unsweetened milk
- $\frac{1}{2}$ cup unsalted pecans
- $\frac{1}{4}$ scoop vanilla protein powder
- 1 tsp granulated sweetener
- $\frac{1}{2}$ tsp vanilla extract
- $\frac{1}{2}$ tsp ground nutmeg
- $\frac{1}{4}$ tsp allspice
- $\frac{1}{4}$ tsp kosher salt

Instructions:

1. Use the high setting to blend all ingredients to a smooth consistency
2. Strain the mixture with a nut-milk bag
3. Chill and serve!

Nutritional Information:

Calories 118

Fat 8g

Carbs. 3.6g

Protein 8.7g

"Bro-tein" Brunch Kickstart

Prep time: 15 min., cook time: 0 min., total time: 15 min.

Serves: 6

Ingredients:

- 8 oz. Cream cheese
- 3 oz. Canned pumpkin
- $\frac{1}{2}$ cup heavy cream, whipped
- $\frac{1}{2}$ tsp salt
- 1 tsp. liquid stevia
- 1 tsp. vanilla extract
- $\frac{1}{4}$ oz. Cacao Nibs
- 2 large eggs, cracked

Instructions:

1. Smoothly blend the cream cheese and pumpkin
2. Add the remaining ingredients; blend till fluffy (about 5 minutes)
3. Taste and if need be, adjust the sweetener
4. Distribute into serving glasses, top with the nibs
5. Refrigerate and serve when cool!

Nutritional Information:

    Calories 221

    Fat 20.1g

    Carbs. 3.5g

    Protein 7.1g

Jelly Creamy Popsicles

Prep time: 30 min., cook time: 0 min., total time: 30 min.

Serves: 3

Ingredients:

- $\frac{1}{2}$ cup heavy cream, whipped
- $\frac{1}{2}$ tbsp. Sugar-free vanilla syrup
- $\frac{1}{2}$ small Jello box
- 3 eggs
- 2 oz. cheddar cheese
- $\frac{1}{8}$ cup cocoa powder

Instructions:

1. Blend all the ingredients on high setting till they are well combined
2. Place five mini-cupcake liners in your cupcake pan
3. Split equal portions of the batter into each liner till half-full
4. Freeze for 30 minutes; serve

Nutritional Information:

Calories 294

Fat 19.2g

Carbs. 9.1g

Protein 12.3g

You May Also Like ...

Book Cover	Book Title	Purchase Link
	Keto Desserts Cookbook 2019 *Easy, Quick and Tasty High-Fat Low-Carb Ketogenic Treats to Try from No-bake Energy Bomblets to Sugar-Free Creamsicle Melts and beyond*	**Buy on Amazon**
	Keto Diet for Beginners 2020 *The Definitive Ketogenic Diet Guide to Kick-start High Level Fat burning, Weight Loss & Healthy Lifestyle in 2020 and Beyond.*	**Buy on Amazon**
	Keto Breakfast Cookbook *Simple No-Mess, No-Fuss Ketogenic Meals to Prepare, Boost Morning Metabolism and Ramp Up Your Energy!*	**Buy on Amazon**
	Keto Lunch Cookbook *Easy Ketogenic Recipes for Work and School; Low Carb Meals to Prep, Grab and Go	With Q&A, Tips, and More..*	**Buy on Amazon**

Note that the Kindle Editions of these books will be made available to you for **FREE** when you get the paperback editions from the Amazon USA store

INDEX

Teresa Baker

73290757R00068

Made in the
USA
Middletown, DE